Siri Hustvedt

Siri Hustvedt's first novel, *The Blindfold*, was published by Sceptre in 1993 and her second, *The Enchantment of Lily Dahl*, followed in 1997. Her third novel, *What I Loved*, was published in 2003 to great acclaim and was an international bestseller. It was followed in 2009 by *The Sorrows of an American* and in 2011 by *The Summer Without Men*. She is also the author of *Reading to You*, a poetry collection, and three collections of essays, *Yonder*, *Mysteries of the Rectangle: Essays on Painting* and *A Plea for Eros*. She lives in Brooklyn, New York, with her husband Paul Auster.

'A personal investigation, a philosophical inquiry, and a pithy, compacted consideration of how both psychiatry and neurology have evolved in the last two centuries ... Fastidious yet engaged, intimate yet detached, Hustvedt's exploration of mind and body embraces material that is inter-disciplinary, complex and contentious. Her clean intelligence is equal to the challenge ... She brings both knowledge and an artist's insight to her discussion of memory, language, personal identity. Readers of Oliver Sacks will rate this book highly'   Hilary Mantel, *Guardian*

'An invigorating antidote to the emotional squelchiness which too often inhabits misery memoirs and illness narratives. Hustvedt is a calm traveller on the storm-tossed seas of the self. If her odyssey provides no ready answers and immediate cures, it deepens understanding.'   Lisa Appignanesi, *Independent*

'Hustvedt compellingly illustrates both the fragmented nature of her treatment, with the fields of psychiatry, neurology and psychoanalysis offering up conflicting views, and the difficulty of making a conclusive diagnosis ... what gives the book its originality is that she wavers on the edge of the various disciplines, preferring her own imaginative, deeply personal reflections to the potential certainty that might be offered by doctors'
Lorna Bradbury, *Daily Telegraph*

'The product of voracious reading and deep thought, and you register its author's sanity in every sentence. If she has not been able to provide as many answers as she might have liked, it is not for want of trying, for she asks all the right questions ... along the way she thinks, long and hard, about illness: where it begins, and where it ends; its impact on personality, and personality's impact on it.'   Rachel Cooke, *Observer*

'Armed with her great gift for elucidation, the novelist and essayist Siri Hustvedt has omnivorously devoured and digested complex debates from neuroscience, psychiatry, philosophy and psycho-analysis and journeyed into the mind/body problem. In *The Shaking Woman*, her quest to understand her own mysterious troubles becomes a brilliant illumination for us all.'

George Makari M.D.

'I was very struck by Siri Hustvedt's *The Shaking Woman or A History of My Nerves*. Not only does it demonstrate nearly complete mastery (by a non-specialist) of the highly special-ized field of neuropsychiatry, it also displays greater under-standing of the underlying philosophical and historical issues that are at stake in this field than is displayed by most of my colleagues. I recommend this highly unusual book unequivo-cally and most enthusiastically.'

Mark Solms

'That Siri Hustvedt is a splendid writer is well known. The news is that life conspired to have her seek a working mastery of neuroscience. In her wonderful new book, part memoir, part mystery story, she explains this unexpected turn of events and offers the reader a wealth of valuable facts along with personal perspectives on the neuroscientific scene. Not surprisingly, the book is a pleasure to read.'

Antonio Damasio

'It brings together an extraordinary double story: that of Hustvedt's own odyssey of discovery, and of that point where brain and mind, neurology and psychiatry, come together in the realm of neuropsychoanalysis. The odyssey has not cured her, nor led to a conclusion – but Hustvedt's erudite book deepens one's wonder about the relation of body and mind.' Oliver Sacks

THE SHAKING
WOMAN

or

A HISTORY
OF
MY NERVES

SIRI HUSTVEDT

SCEPTRE

First published in the United States in 2010 by Henry Holt and Company

First published in Great Britain in 2010 by Sceptre
An imprint of Hodder & Stoughton
An Hachette UK company

First published in paperback in 2011

1

A CIP catalogue record for this title is available
from the British Library.

ISBN 978 0 340 99877 9

Printed and bound by Clays Ltd, St Ives plc

Hodder & Stoughton policy is to use papers that are natural,
renewable and recyclable products and made from wood grown
in sustainable forests. The logging and manufacturing processes
are expected to conform to the environmental regulations
of the country of origin.

Hodder & Stoughton Ltd
338 Euston Road
London NW1 3BH

www.hodder.co.uk

I felt a Cleaving in my Mind—

As if my Brain had split—

I tried to match it—Seam by Seam—

But could not make it fit.

EMILY DICKINSON

WHEN MY FATHER DIED, I was at home in Brooklyn, but only days before I had been sitting beside his bed in a nursing home in Northfield, Minnesota. Although he was weak in body, his mind remained sharp, and I remember that we talked and even laughed, though I can't recall the content of our last conversation. I can, however, clearly see the room where he lived at the end of his life. My three sisters, my mother, and I had hung pictures on the wall and bought a pale green bedspread to make the room less stark. There was a vase of flowers on the windowsill. My father had emphysema, and we knew he would not last long. My sister Liv, who lives in Minnesota, was the only daughter with him on the final day. His lung had collapsed for the second time, and the doctor understood that he would not survive another intervention. While he was still conscious, but unable to speak, my mother called her three daughters in New York City, one by one, so we could talk to him on the telephone. I distinctly remember that I paused to think about what I should say to him. I had the curious thought that I should not utter something stupid at such a moment, that I should choose my words carefully. I wanted to say something memorable—an absurd thought, because my father's memory would soon be snuffed out with the rest of him. But when my mother put the telephone to his ear, all I could do was choke out the words "I love you so much." Later, my mother told me that when he heard my voice, he smiled.

That night I dreamed that I was with him and he reached out for me, that I fell toward him for an embrace, and then, before he could put his arms around me, I woke up. My sister Liv called me the next morning to say that our father was dead. Immediately after that conversation, I stood up from the chair where I had been sitting, climbed the stairs to my study, and sat down to write his eulogy. My father had asked me to do it. Several weeks earlier, when I was sitting beside him in the nursing home, he had mentioned "three points" he wanted me to take down. He didn't say, "I want you to include them in the text you will write for my funeral." He didn't have to. It was understood. When the time came, I didn't weep. I wrote. At the funeral I delivered my speech in a strong voice, without tears.

TWO AND A HALF YEARS LATER, I gave another talk in honor of my father. I was back in my hometown, in Minnesota, standing under a blue May sky on the St. Olaf College campus, just beyond the old building that housed the Norwegian Department, where my father had been a professor for almost forty years. The department had planted a memorial pine tree with a small plaque beneath it that read, LLOYD HUSTVEDT (1922–2004). While I'd been writing this second text, I'd had a strong sensation of hearing my father's voice. He wrote excellent and often very funny speeches, and as I composed I imagined that I had caught some of his humor in my sentences. I even used the phrase "Were my father here today, he might have said . . ." Confident and armed with index cards, I looked out at the fifty or so friends and colleagues of my father's who had gathered around the memorial Norway spruce, launched into my first sentence, and began to shudder violently from the neck down. My arms flapped. My knees knocked. I shook as if I were having a seizure. Weirdly, my voice wasn't affected. It didn't change at all. Astounded by what was happening to me and terrified that I would fall over, I managed to keep my balance and continue, despite the fact that the cards in my hands were flying back and forth in front of me. When the speech ended, the shaking stopped. I looked down at my legs. They had turned a deep red with a bluish cast.

My mother and sisters were startled by the mysterious bodily transformation that had taken place within me. They had seen me speak in public many times, sometimes in front of hundreds of people. Liv said she had wanted to go over and put her arms around me to hold me up. My mother said she had felt as if she were looking at an electrocution. It appeared that some unknown force had suddenly taken over my body and decided I needed a good, sustained jolting. Once before, during the summer of 1982, I'd felt as if some superior power picked me up and tossed me about as if I were a doll. In an art gallery in Paris, I suddenly felt my left arm jerk upward and slam me backward into the wall. The whole event lasted no more than a few seconds. Not long after that, I felt euphoric, filled with supernatural joy, and then came the violent migraine that lasted for almost a year, the year of Fiorinal, Inderal, cafergot, Elavil, Tofranil, and Mellaril, of a sleeping-drug cocktail I took in the doctor's office in hopes that I would wake up headache-free. No such luck. Finally, that same neurologist sent me to the hospital and put me on the antipsychotic drug Thorazine. Those eight stuporous days in the neurology ward with my old but surprisingly agile roommate, a stroke victim, who every night was strapped to her bed with a restraint sweetly known as a Posey, and who every night defied the nurses by escaping her fetters and fleeing down the corridor, those strange drugged days, punctuated by visits from young men in white coats who held up pencils for me to identify, asked me the day and the year and the name of the president, pricked me with little needles—Can you feel this?—and the rare wave through the door from the Headache Czar himself, Dr. C., a man who mostly ignored me and seemed irritated that I didn't cooperate and get well, have stayed with me as a time of the blackest of all black comedies. Nobody really knew what was wrong with me. My doctor gave it a name—*vascular migraine syndrome*—but why I had become a vomiting, miserable, flattened, frightened ENORMOUS headache, a Humpty Dumpty after his fall, no one could say.

My travels in the worlds of neurology, psychiatry, and psychoanalysis began well before my stint in Mount Sinai Medical Center. I have suffered from migraines since childhood and have long been curious about my own aching head, my dizziness, my divine lifting feelings, my sparklers and black holes, and my single visual hallucination of a little pink man and a pink ox on the floor of my bedroom. I had been reading about these mysteries for many years before I had my shaking fit that afternoon in Northfield. But my investigations intensified when I decided to write a novel in which I would have to impersonate a psychiatrist and psychoanalyst, a man I came to think of as my imaginary brother, Erik Davidsen. Brought up in Minnesota by parents very much like mine, he was the boy never born to the Hustvedt family. To be Erik, I threw myself into the convolutions of psychiatric diagnoses and the innumerable mental disorders that afflict human beings. I studied pharmacology and familiarized myself with the various classes of drugs. I bought a book with sample tests for the New York State psychiatric boards and practiced taking them. I read more psychoanalysis and countless memoirs of mental illness. I found myself fascinated by neuroscience, attended a monthly lecture on brain science at the New York

Psychoanalytic Institute, and was invited to become a member of a discussion group devoted to a new field: neuropsychoanalysis.

In that group, neuroscientists, neurologists, psychiatrists, and psychoanalysts sought a common ground that might bring together the insights of analysis with the most recent brain research. I bought myself a rubber brain, familiarized myself with its many parts, listened intently, and read more. In fact, I read obsessively, as my husband has told me repeatedly. He has even suggested that my rapacious reading resembles an addiction. Then I signed up as a volunteer at the Payne Whitney Psychiatric Clinic and began teaching a writing class to the patients there every week. At the hospital, I found myself close to particular human beings who suffered from complex illnesses that sometimes bore little resemblance to the descriptions cataloged in the *Diagnostic and Statistical Manual of Mental Disorders* (usually referred to as the *DSM*). By the time I shook in front of my father's tree, I had been steeped in the world of the brain/mind for years. What began with curiosity about the mysteries of my own nervous system had developed into an overriding passion. Intellectual curiosity about one's own illness is certainly born of a desire for mastery. If I couldn't cure myself, perhaps I could at least begin to understand myself.

EVERY SICKNESS HAS an alien quality, a feeling of invasion and loss of control that is evident in the language we use about it. No one says, "I am cancer" or even "I am cancerous," despite the fact that there is no intruding virus or bac-

6

teria; it's the body's own cells that have run amok. One *has* cancer. Neurological and psychiatric illnesses are different, however, because they often attack the very source of what one imagines is one's self. "He's an epileptic" doesn't sound strange to us. In the psychiatric clinic, the patients often say, "Well, you see, I'm bipolar" or "I'm schizophrenic." The illness and the self are fully identified in these sentences. The shaking woman felt like me and not like me at the same time. From the chin up, I was my familiar self. From the neck down, I was a shuddering stranger. Whatever had happened to me, whatever name would be assigned to my affliction, my strange seizure must have had an emotional component that was somehow connected to my father. The problem was that I hadn't *felt* emotional. I had felt entirely calm and reasonable. Something seemed to have gone terribly wrong with me, but what exactly? I decided to go in search of the shaking woman.

PHYSICIANS HAVE BEEN PUZZLING over convulsions like mine for centuries. Many diseases can make you shudder, but it's not always easy to separate one from the other. From Hippocrates onward, making a diagnosis has meant herding a cluster of symptoms under a single name. Epilepsy is the most famous of all the shaking illnesses. Had I been a patient of the Greek physician Galen, who ministered to the emperor Marcus Aurelius and whose copious writings influenced medical history for hundreds of years, he would have diagnosed me with a convulsive illness, but he would have ruled out epilepsy. For Galen, epilepsy not

7

only caused convulsions of the entire body, it interrupted "leading functions"—awareness and speech.[1] Although there were popular beliefs among the Greeks that gods and ghosts could make you shake, most physicians took a naturalist view of the phenomenon, and it wasn't until the rise of Christianity that tremors and the supernatural were bound together with bewildering intimacy. Nature, God, and the devil could wrack your body, and medical experts struggled to distinguish among causes. How could you separate an act of nature from a divine intervention or a demonic possession? Saint Teresa of Avila's paroxysmal agonies and blackouts, her visions and transports were mystical flights toward God, but the girls in Salem who writhed and shook were the victims of witches. In *A Modest Inquiry into the Nature of Witchcraft,* John Hale describes the fits of the tormented children and then pointedly adds that their extreme sufferings were "beyond the power of any epileptic fits or natural disease to effect."[2] If my tremulous episode had occurred during the witch madness in Salem, the consequences might have been dire. Surely I would have looked like a woman possessed. But, more important, had I been steeped in the religious beliefs of the age, as I most likely would have been, the weird sensation that some external power had entered my body to cause the shudder probably would have been enough to convince me that I had indeed been hexed.

In New York City in 2006 no sane doctor would have sent me to an exorcist, and yet confusion about diagnosis is common. The frames for viewing convulsive illness may have changed, but understanding what had happened to me would not be a simple matter. I could go to a neurologist to see if I had come down with epilepsy, although my past experience in the ward at Mount Sinai Hospital had left me wary of the doctors in charge of investigating nervous systems. I knew that in order to be diagnosed with the disease, I needed to have had at least *two* seizures. I believed I had had one genuine seizure before my intractable migraine. The second one looked suspicious to me. Uncontrollable shaking can occur in some seizures. My shaking was on both sides of my body—and I had *talked* throughout the fit. How many people *talk* through a seizure? Also, I had had no aura, no warning that some neurological event was in the making, as I often do for migraine, and it had come and gone with the speech about my dead father. Because of my history, I knew that a careful neurologist would do an EEG, an electroencephalogram. I'd have to sit with gooey electrodes clamped onto my scalp for quite a while, and my guess is that the doctor would find nothing. Of course, many people suffer from seizures that are not detected by standard tests, so the physician would have to do more tests. Unless I kept shaking, a diagnosis might not be forthcoming. I could float in the limbo of an unknown affliction.

I had puzzled for some time over my shaking when a possible answer announced itself. It didn't appear slowly but came all at once as an epiphany. I was sitting in my regular seat at the monthly neuroscience lecture, and I remembered a brief conversation I had had with a psychiatrist who had been sitting behind me at an earlier talk. I'd asked her where she worked and what she did, and she'd told me she was on the staff in a hospital, where she saw mostly "conversion patients." "The neurologists don't know what to do with them," she'd said, "so they send them to me." *That could be it!* I thought. My fit had been *hysterical.* This ancient word has been mostly dropped from current medical discourse and replaced by *conversion disorder,* but lying beneath the newer term is the old one, haunting it like a ghost.

Nearly every time the word *hysteria* is used now in newspapers or magazines, the writer points out that the root comes from the Greek for "womb." Its origin as a purely female problem connected to reproductive organs serves to warn readers that the word itself reflects an ancient bias against women, but its history is far more complicated than misogyny. Galen believed that hysteria was an illness that beset unmarried and widowed women who were deprived of sexual intercourse but that it wasn't madness, because it didn't necessarily involve psychological impairments. Ancient doctors were well aware that epileptic fits and hysterical fits could look alike, and that it was essential to try to distinguish between the two. As it turns out, the confusion has never disappeared. The fifteenth-century physician Antonius Guainerius believed that vapors rising from the uterus caused hysteria and that hysteria could be distinguished from epilepsy because the hysterical person would remember everything that had happened during the fit.[3] The great seventeenth-century English doctor Thomas Willis dispensed with the uterus as the offending organ and located both hysteria and epilepsy in the brain. But Willis's thought didn't rule the day. There were those who believed that the two were merely different forms of the same disease. The Swiss physician Samuel Auguste David Tissot (1728–1797), who has remained part of medical history mostly for his widely published treatise on the dangers of masturbation, maintained that the two illnesses were distinct, despite the fact that there were epilepsies that originated in the uterus.[4] From ancient times through the eighteenth century, hysteria was regarded as a convulsive illness that originated somewhere in the body—in the uterus or the brain or a limb—and the people suffering from it weren't considered insane. It is safe to say that if any one of the doctors above had witnessed my convulsive speech, he might have diagnosed me with hysteria. My higher functions weren't interrupted; I remembered everything about my fit; and, of course, I was a woman with a potentially vaporous or disturbed uterus.

It's interesting to ask when hysteria became an illness associated exclusively with the mind. In ordinary speech we use the word *hysteria* to indicate a person's excitability or excessive emotion. It conjures up a screaming out-of-control person, usually a woman. Whatever was happening to my arms, legs, and torso, my mind was all right, and I spoke calmly. I wasn't hysterical in that sense. Today, conversion disorder is classified as a psychiatric, not a neurological disorder, which explains why we connect it to mental problems. In the *DSM,* now in its fourth edition, conversion disorder is included among the *somatoform* disorders—disturbances of the body and physical sensations.[5] But in the last forty years, the term for and classification of the illness has changed several times. In the first *DSM* (1952) it was called *conversion reaction*. The *DSM-II* (1968) grouped it with *dissociation* disorders and identified it as *hysterical neurosis, conversion type*. In 1968, the authors were apparently eager to reinstate the roots of the illness by bringing back the word *hysteria*. *Dissociation* is a very broad term used in different ways to indicate some form of distance from or disruption of ordinary selfhood. For example, when a person has an out-of-body experience, he is said to be in a dissociated state; someone who is plagued by a sense that he or the world isn't real would also be called dissociated. By the time the *DSM-III* (1980) came out, the word *hysterical* had vanished, and the term had been changed to *conversion disorder,* a somatoform problem, which was left unchanged in the *DSM-IV*. The current manual of the World Health Organization, the *ICD-10* (1992), however, disagrees. There it's called *dissociative (conversion) disorder*. If this sounds confusing, it is. The authors of psychiatric diagnostic texts have obviously been uncertain about what to do with hysteria.

There is some general agreement, however. Conversion symptoms often mimic neurological symptoms: paralyses; seizures; difficulty walking, swallowing, or speaking; blindness; and deafness. But when a neurologist investigates, he won't be able to find anything that would normally cause these problems. So, for example, if some wandering neurologist had happened to give me an EEG while I was shaking in front of the tree, hysterical convulsions wouldn't have been recorded on it, but epileptic shudders might have been. At the same time, hysterics are not malingerers. They can't help what's happening to them and aren't faking their illnesses. Also, the symptoms can and often do resolve themselves spontaneously. The big caveat is that, as the *DSM* authors note, "Caution must be exercised."[6] In other words, if I had gone to a psychiatrist he would have had to be careful about me. An unidentified neurological illness might have been hiding under my symptoms that wouldn't show up on any tests. He'd have to be confident that my shakes were too odd for epilepsy before he made the diagnosis. And the problem goes both ways. Carl Basil, a pharmacologist at Columbia University, tells the story of a patient who watched the place where he worked burn down and "suddenly became paralyzed on the right side as if he had a stroke."[7] In fact, the man had had a "conversion reaction," which vanished with his shock. The issue is further riddled by the fact that people who suffer from epilepsy are far more likely to have hysterical seizures than people who do not have the disease. In one paper I read, the authors stated that between 10 and 60 percent of people with psychogenic nonepileptic seizures (PNES) have comordid epilepsy.[8] This contemporary dilemma of identification sounds a lot like the difficulties physicians have had throughout the ages separating epilepsy from hysteria. The question has always been, A woman is shaking. Why?

For years in the late twentieth century, physicians blithely threw around the phrase "no organic cause." Hysteria was a psychic illness with no *organic* cause. People found themselves paralyzed, blind, and convulsing without any organic cause? How could that be? Unless you believed that ghosts, spirits, or demons swooped in from heaven or hell to take control of a person's body, how could it be argued that this wasn't an *organic, physical* phenomenon? Even the current *DSM* acknowledges the problem, stating that the difference between mental and physical is "a reductionistic anachronism of mind/body dualism."[9] That split has been with us in the West at least since Plato. The idea that we are made of two stuffs, not one, that mind isn't matter, continues to be part of many people's thinking about the world. Certainly the experience of living in my own head has a magical quality. How do I see and feel and think, and exactly what is my mind? Is my mind the same thing as my brain? How can the human experience originate in white and gray matter? What is organic and nonorganic?

Last year, I heard a man talking on the radio about life with his schizophrenic son. Like many patients, his son had trouble staying on his medicine. After hospitalizations, he would return home, stop taking the drug he had been prescribed, and collapse again. It's a story I've heard often from the patients I teach in the hospital, but with each person the reasons for going off the medicine are different. One patient got horribly fat from an antipsychotic, and it made him miserable; another felt dead inside; another was furious with her mother and stopped out of spite. The father on the radio made a point of saying, "Schizophrenia is an *organic brain disease.*" I understood why he said it. No doubt his son's doctors had told him this or he had read articles about the illness that referred to it in this way, and it comforted him, made him feel that as a father he was not responsible for his child's illness, that the boy's environment had played no role. The genetic mystery of schizophrenia may one day be solved, but for now it remains unknown. If one identical twin suffers from the disease, there's a 50 percent chance that the other will. That's high but not determining. There have to be other factors at work, environmental factors, which might be anything from poisons in the air to parental neglect. Too often, people prefer easy answers. In the current cultural climate, *organic brain disease* has a reassuring sound. My son isn't mad; he has something wrong with his brain.

But there is no quick route out of the psyche/soma trap. Peter Rudnytsky, a prominent scholar of psychoanalysis, discusses Otto Rank, a psychoanalyst in Freud's circle, who probably suffered from manic depression. He notes that because manic depression is now known to be an "organic" illness, Rank's mood swings can't be construed as a taint on his "character."[10] Manic depression, also known as bipolar disorder, does run in families, and the genetic component seems to be considerably higher than in schizophrenia. And yet, Rudnytsky implies that there are nonorganic states that might be attributable to character flaws. This raises a question: What is character? Isn't character the sum of our parts, and aren't those parts organic? And if not, what is psychic and what is somatic?

The problem is that the phrase *organic brain disease* doesn't mean much. There are no lesions or holes in the brain tissue of schizophrenics or manic-depressives, no virus eating away at their cortices. There are changes in brain activity that can be detected by the new technology of brain scans. But then there are brain changes when we are sad or happy or lustful, too. All of these human states are physical. And what is a disease exactly? In *Campbell's Psychiatric Dictionary*, I found this remark from Culver and Gert's *Philosophy in Medicine*: "Illness and disease are closely related, but diseases are ontologically more robust than just an illness."[11] A disease, in other words, has more there there, more *being* than an illness. Not long ago, a friend of mine showed me a book called *Living Well with Migraine Disease and Headaches*. I was amazed. In my earlier travels from one neurologist to another, migraine was never referred to as a *disease*. Obviously it had gained new status, had attained a more "robust" existence since 1982. Is conversion disorder, unlike schizophrenia or manic depression, a psychic phenomenon? Is a psyche different from a brain?

Sigmund Freud was the first to use the word *conversion* in the book he published with Josef Breuer, *Studies on Hysteria* (1893): "For the sake of brevity, we adopt the term 'conversion' to designate the transformation of psychical excitement into the chronic somatic symptoms, which is so characteristic of hysteria."[12] What did Freud mean by this? Did he believe that psychical excitement was a nonbiological entity? Freud was a man steeped in the philosophy and science of his time. As a medical student, he pursued his degree but took additional classes in philosophy and zoology. In the summer of 1876, Freud received a grant to go to the

Zoological Experimental Station at Trieste, where he spent his time dissecting eels, studying their histological structure, and looking for testes that no one had ever been able to find. It seems that the gonadic structure of eels had been puzzling interested parties since Aristotle. Freud's results were inconclusive, but his research was part of the journey that would eventually end with an answer to the question. After three years of medical school, he settled on neurology as his main interest and spent six years studying nerve cells in the physiology laboratory of Ernst Wilhelm von Brücke. He concentrated on the visible material of the nervous system. The first book Freud published was *On Aphasia: A Critical Study*. Aphasia—the word is derived from the Greek for "speechless"—refers to language problems in patients who have brain damage. Every aspect of language can be affected. Some patients understand words but can't produce them. Some can't comprehend what is being said to them or can't register whole sentences. Others know what they want to say but can't retrieve the phonemes to utter it. Although not given great attention at the time, much of what Freud argued in that book remains valuable. He insisted that although brain processes could be localized—certain parts of the brain were responsible for different human behaviors, such as language—they were not static but were dynamic moving pathways in the brain. This is unquestionably true. His position on the connection between mind and matter was subtle. He was neither a reductionist nor a dualist: "The psychic is, therefore, a process parallel to the physiological, a dependent concomitant."[13]

Freud remained a materialist all his life. He did not truck with misty notions about souls, spirits, or psyches detached from physical processes. One depended on the other. At the same time, following Kant, he did not believe that it was possible to know things-in-themselves. Our access to the world comes only through our perceptions of it, he argued. And yet, I'm always running into people who treat Freud almost as if he had been a mystic, a man whose ideas bear no relation to physical realities, a kind of monster of mirage who derailed modernity by feeding all kinds of nonsense to a gullible public until his thought was finally shattered by a new scientific psychiatry founded on the wonders of pharmacology. How did a scientist acquire this reputation?

Not long after he published *Studies on Hysteria* with Breuer, Freud embarked on what was later called his *Project for a Scientific Psychology,* an attempt to attach his insights about how the mind works to his knowledge of neurology and create a biological model founded on brain stuff— neurons. After a period of feverish writing, he realized that not enough was known about neural processes to produce such a map, and he put his *Project* aside. The father of psychoanalysis then made his fateful turn toward a purely psychological explanation of the mind, although he never abandoned the idea that sometime in the future, scientists would be able to ground his ideas in actual brain functions. In his history of psychoanalysis, *Revolution in Mind,* George Makari offers a pithy assessment of the problem Freud and many others working in neurology, psychology, and biophysics faced: "One could not glibly say a nerve housed a word or an idea."[14] Freud had thoughts about how this connection worked, but he couldn't begin to prove he was right.

LET US SAY THAT after my imaginary visit to the neurologist turned up nothing of interest, I decided to see a psychoanalyst. Although American psychiatry was once heavily influenced by psychoanalysis, the two disciplines have grown further and further apart, especially since the 1970s. Many psychiatrists have little or no knowledge of psychoanalysis, which has become increasingly marginalized in the culture. Large numbers of American psychiatrists now leave most of the talk to social workers and stick to writing prescriptions. Pharmacology dominates. Nevertheless, there are still many psychoanalysts practicing around the world, and it's a discipline I've been fascinated by since I was sixteen and first read Freud. I've never been in psychoanalysis, but at a couple of junctures in my life I've considered becoming an analyst, and in order to do that I would have to be analyzed myself. I was in psychotherapy once, briefly, and it was very helpful, but I've come to understand that some part of me is afraid of an analysis. That fear is difficult to articulate because I'm not sure where it comes from. I have a vague sense that there are hidden recesses of my personality that I am reluctant to penetrate. Maybe that's the part of me that shook. The intimacy of the dialogue between analyst and patient is also rather frightening. Frankly, saying *everything* on my mind has a terrifying ring to it. My imaginary analyst is a man. I choose a man because he

would be a paternal creature, an echo of my father, who is
the ghost somehow involved in my shaking.

After listening to my story, my analyst would surely
want to find out about my father's death and my relationship to him. My mother would come into the dialogue as
well, and no doubt my husband and daughter and sisters
and all the people who are important to me. We would talk,
and through the exchange the two of us would hope to discover why a speech I delivered in front of a pine tree turned
me into a shivering wreck. Of course, it has to be acknowledged that talking wasn't my problem. Even while I was in
the grip of the thing, I was fluent. My pathology lay somewhere else, beneath or to the side of language, depending on
the spatial metaphor. The psychoanalytic word for my difficulty might be *repression.* I had repressed something, which
had then burst out of my unconscious as a hysterical symptom. Indeed, my dilemma would look classic to a Freudian
analyst. I would, of course, tell my phantom analyst that I
had visited a neurologist and wasn't an epileptic, and from
that moment on, he wouldn't spend much time worrying
about my *brain.* Although Freud was fascinated by neurons,
my analyst would forget about them and instead help me
dig into my story, and between us we would find a way to
retell it in order to cure me of my symptom. On my way to a
cure, I would fall in love with my analyst. I would go through
transference. Through that love, which might also turn into
hate or indifference or fear, I would transfer to him the feelings I had or have for my father, my mother, or my sisters,
and he, in turn, would have a countertransference, shaped

by his own personal story. We would find ourselves in the grip of ideas, as well as emotions. In the end—there is supposed to be an end—we would have a story about my pseudoseizure, and I would be cured. That is, at least, the ideal narrative of an analysis, which is a peculiar form of storytelling. Freud himself noted the oddness of the enterprise in *Studies on Hysteria*:

> Like other neuropathologists, I was trained to employ local diagnoses and electro-prognosis, and it still strikes me as strange that the case histories I write should read like short stories and that, as one might say, they lack the serious stamp of science. I must console myself with the reflection that the nature of the subject is evidently responsible for this, rather than any preference of my own. The fact is that local diagnosis and electrical reactions lead nowhere in the study of hysteria, whereas a detailed description of mental processes such as we are accustomed to find in the works of imaginative writers enables me, with the use of a few psychological formulas, to obtain at least some kind of insight into the course of that affection.[15]

As a scientist, Freud felt a little queasy about sounding like a fiction writer. Over time, his thoughts about the psychic apparatus would both change and evolve, but he would never be able to sink his theories into the nervous system, where he knew its processes originated. Aphasia was an illness with an identified physiological ground. Damage to particular parts of the brain caused language problems.

When Freud wrote on aphasia, the French scientist Paul Broca and the German scientist Carl Wernicke had already done their groundbreaking work that localized language centers in the brain's left hemisphere. Hysteria, however, was an illness *without* brain lesions. The work of the eminent French neurologist Jean-Martin Charcot, whom Freud knew, translated, studied under, and was deeply influenced by, had made this clear. Working in the Salpêtrière Hospital in Paris, Charcot, like countless physicians before him, struggled to distinguish epileptic seizures from what he called "hystero-epilepsy." Because some genuine epilepsies could also occur without lesions in the brain, a fact discovered through autopsy, Charcot had to make the distinction between the two illnesses on clinical grounds by carefully observing his patients. He categorized diseases like hysteria, which were not caused by anatomical lesions, with the "neuroses." He considered hysteria a neurological, *organic disease,* maintained that it had a hereditary basis, and said it wasn't unique to women. Men could be hysterical, too.

Charcot became interested in the psychological dimension of hysteria when he noticed that a severe fright or powerful emotion could be linked to its symptoms. In such cases, Charcot believed, the shock created an autosuggestion, a form of self-hypnosis in the patient that remained outside his awareness. For example, one of the neurologist's patients, diagnosed with traumatic male hysteria, was a blacksmith who had suffered a burn to his hand and forearm and then weeks later developed contractures in the same part of his body. The theory was that trauma could create an idea that acted on a person's already vulnerable nervous system to create the symptom: a fit; a paralysis; the inability to walk, hear, or see; fugues; or somnambulisms. Furthermore, a doctor could produce the same symptom by hypnotizing the patient and suggesting to him that his hand was paralyzed. Autosuggestion and hypnotic suggestion activated the same physiological areas and so were two forms of the same process. For Charcot, the very fact that a person could be hypnotized meant that he or she was a hysteric. Despite his interest in trauma, Charcot remained committed to a physiological explanation of hysteria.[16]

Pierre Janet, a philosopher and neurologist who was a younger colleague of Charcot's went further than his mentor in exploring the psychic aspects of hysteria. He maintained, as Charcot had, that hysteria could begin with a shock—a carriage accident, for example—and that the person need not have been physically hurt in the crash. It was enough, Janet argued, for him to have the idea that "the wheel passed over his leg" for the limb to become paralyzed.[17] Janet was the first to use the word *dissociation* in relation to hysteria. He defined it as a division among "systems of ideas and functions that constitute the personality."[18] Ideas, for Janet, weren't disembodied thoughts but were part of psychobiological systems that included emotions, memories, sensations, and behaviors. In a series of lectures Janet delivered at Harvard in 1906, he argued that hysteria was defined by "suggestion," which was "a too powerful idea that acts on the body in an abnormal way."[19] The horrible idea of the carriage accident becomes dissociated within the person:

"Things happen as if an idea, a partial system of thoughts, emancipated itself, became independent and developed itself on its own account. The result is, on the one hand, that it develops far too much, and, on the other hand, that consciousness appears no longer to control it."[20] Hysteria, then, is a systemic divide that allows a renegade part of the self to wander off unguided.

Janet tells the story of Irene, an impoverished young woman of twenty, who watched her beloved mother die a slow, agonizing death from tuberculosis. After weeks of sitting by the sickbed, Irene noticed that her mother had stopped breathing and desperately tried to revive her. During those efforts, her mother's corpse fell to the floor, and it took all of Irene's strength to lift the body back onto the bed. After her mother's funeral, Irene began to relive the death in trances, acting out its horror in great detail or telling it over and over again. After these reenactments, she would return to normal consciousness and behave as if nothing had happened. Irene's relatives reported that the girl seemed weirdly unconcerned about her mother's death. Indeed, she seemed to have forgotten about it. Irene herself expressed surprise and asked when and how her mother had died. "There is something I don't understand," she said. "Why, loving her as I did, do I not feel more sorrow for her death? I can't grieve; I feel as if her absence were nothing to me, as if she were traveling and would soon come back."[21]

I was struck by this passage. I wondered if there was a similar blankness in myself. Should I have grieved more for someone I had loved so much? For many months after he died, I dreamed that my father was still alive. I had been wrong about his dying; he wasn't dead at all. Irene sat by helplessly as her mother died. When my father was dying, I spent hours with him in a chair beside his bed. Oxygen helped him breathe, and he could no longer get out of bed without help. After his lung collapsed, the doctors revived him by drilling a hole into his chest and reinflating the lung. I remember the hole. I remember his gray face in the hospital in Minneapolis, the ugly fluorescent light in the small room, and the groaning old man in the bed next to him behind a curtain. I remember that when my father was able to return to the nursing home, he smiled as he was wheeled into the narrow room and said, "It's good to be home, even though it's not really home." He and I talked a lot in the days before he died, about many things, and as we talked, I kept telling myself to expect his death, to prepare for it. He was eighty-one years old and had lived a long life. People don't live forever. We all die. I fed myself the usual platitudes, and I thought the stories I told myself worked, but I now think I may have been wrong.

Janet coined the phrase *la belle indifférence,* which is still used. It is generally understood to be a strange lack of concern about one's own illness and is specifically connected to conversion disorder or hysteria. An example given in a primer for students studying for the psychiatric boards is illustrative: After his mother dies in his home country, Mexico, a man now living in the United States suddenly goes blind. No physical cause can be located, and he seems oddly unconcerned about the fact that he can't see. His blithe attitude to a condition so dramatic is a hint that he may be a conversion patient.[22] In Irene's case, the indifference was connected to the traumatic event itself. Was this my problem? Why, loving him as I did, do I not feel more sorrow? Janet would have said that the grief had gone into a hidden part of me. Freud would have understood my problem as an efficient way to protect myself from what I couldn't acknowledge. The hysterical shaking served a concealing, useful purpose.

And yet, a curious indifference is also seen in neurological patients who have *visible* lesions in their brains. People with Anton's syndrome, after suffering some devastating neurological event, such as a stroke, lose their sight but insist that they can see. Anton's is part of a much broader phenomenon called anosognosia—denial of illness. In his book *Altered Egos*, Todd Feinberg describes a woman, Lizzy, who had had strokes in both occipital lobes of her brain, where the primary visual cortex is located, and had become totally blind. "She might deny her blindness, and later admit it," he writes, "but never did she seem to act as if her visual impairment was of any concern. She talked throughout the interview and acted as if she had not a care in the world."[23] Lizzy vacillated between knowing and not knowing that she couldn't see, but even when she seemed to know, her attitude was consistent. She didn't appear to *care*. Two people have gone blind. One person's visual cortex is intact; the other's is damaged. One is a psychiatric case, another a neurological one, but both display an uncanny lack of distress about their plight. Is their nonchalance connected? Aren't they both in some way dissociated from what has happened to them? Could their similar attitudes be considered repression, to use the psychoanalytic term? Is the indifference psychological in the first case but neurological in the second? Of course, not all people who have lesions in their primary visual cortex and go blind deny being blind; only *some* people. And not all people suffering from conversion disorder have *la belle indifférence*. But Irene, the fictitious Mexican, Lizzy, and I may have something in common: a grieving problem. Irene was so traumatized by her mother's death that some fragment of her self repeated the circumstances of that demise over and over again, while another part felt nothing. Did I, too, have a kind of double consciousness—a shuddering person and a cool one?

ABOUT SIX MONTHS AFTER my shaking episode, I gave a lecture at New York Presbyterian Hospital as part of a series of talks in Columbia University's Program in Narrative Medicine, run by Rita Charon. Charon is a physician who also has a PhD in literature. Her mission is to bring storytelling back to medical practice. Without it, she argues, the reality of a single person's suffering is lost and medicine suffers. Her distinction between nonstory and story is one of focus: "Nonnarrative knowledge attempts to illuminate the universal by transcending the particular; narrative knowledge, by looking closely at individual human beings grappling with the conditions of life, attempts to illuminate the universals of the human condition by revealing the particular."[24] In my talk, I described my tree-commemoration fit and used three figments—a psychiatrist, a psychoanalyst, and a neurologist—to illustrate how a single paroxysmal event might be construed differently, depending on your field of expertise. Disciplinary lenses inevitably inform perception. There I was giving another speech, this time in front of psychiatrists, psychoanalysts, and doctoral students in literature, and I was telling them about my shuddering. Before the lecture, a thought entered my mind: *What if I shake again?* At the very beginning, I felt my hands tremble. That was familiar, and I didn't think much of it. The more I talked, the more I relaxed. I could feel that the audience was listening. My confession about the shakes had a purpose, and everyone seemed to understand it. The talk went well. Some months later, I gave a shorter version of the same speech at a literary seminar in Key West, Florida. Before that second delivery, I had participated in several panels onstage without a quiver.

On the day in question, I was one of four speakers. A well-known, popular novelist who had appeared on *The Oprah Winfrey Show* went immediately before me. He spoke movingly about his work with female prison inmates. His talk was sad, but it had a happy ending. Despite grotesque manipulations on the part of prison authorities to squelch the writing of the women he had taught, his efforts had triumphed in the end. People jumped to their feet. The applause was loud and long. Now it was my turn to offer up my adventures in the fields of the mind, including my work teaching writing to psychiatric patients in the hospital. I wasn't at all nervous, although I knew that in comparison to the speech that had come before me, mine might seem arcane. My sincerity, however, was beyond question, and I felt good about what I had to say. I walked up to the stage, and the moment I uttered the first word, it happened again. I was shaking in front of hundreds of people. I gripped the podium, but my arms, torso, and legs were shuddering so badly that there was no disguising it. I had managed to push through the first paragraph when I heard someone in a front row say, "She's shaking" and then another person, "I think she's having a seizure." Pressing my hands hard onto the sides of the wooden podium in front of me as the mortifying spasms continued, I told the audience to bear with me, that I was actually going to discuss the shaking a little later in the talk. Again my voice was unaffected, although I spoke too fast, hoping I could catapult myself to the end, which, I was convinced, would also bring the shaking to a halt. My husband (who had not attended the tree ceremony) told me later that he had never witnessed anything like it. Although I had described my earlier fit to him, he hadn't understood how dramatic it had been. He was tempted to rush up onto the stage, grab me, and carry me bodily down the stairs.

But as I talked on, the shuddering began to diminish; not all at once but slowly, gradually my convulsive motion subsided. By the end of the talk, it had left me altogether. The audience was kind. They clapped. A neurologist, a psychiatrist, and a psychotherapist approached me afterward and, to my immense relief, offered not their services but reflections on the content of the speech. Several other people came up to me and told me I was "brave." I didn't feel brave. What was I to do? I hadn't thought I needed an ambulance. I had been confident that the shaking would end when the speech did. The only options were to go on talking or to fall to the floor and admit defeat. A friend, who had been a professor of mine at Columbia University when I was a graduate student and who was also a participant in the seminar, told me afterward that it had been like watching a doctor and a patient in the same body. Indeed, I had been two people that day—a reasonable orator and a woman in the middle of a personal quake. Entirely against my will, I had demonstrated the very pathology I was describing.

For many hours afterward, I felt wobbly and exhausted. My limbs had a flulike soreness, and I was plagued by some dizziness. But above all, what I felt was fear. What if it kept happening? I asked myself whether the fits had been triggered by talking about my father or perhaps simply by anticipating that I was going to talk about him. But then why hadn't I shaken at the Narrative Medicine lecture? Why had I felt so calm before the two episodes? Had the reception given to the popular novelist created a subliminal idea that after his victorious narrative my comments would be disappointing? Had I stayed up too late the night before and drunk too many cups of coffee that morning? I had sat through a lecture on panic attacks given by a pharmacologist in which he had made it clear that vulnerability can be created by certain behaviors. Smokers, for example, are more prone to panic than nonsmokers. I had stopped smoking years before, but caffeine is a stimulant that might have predisposed me to the shakes. Disappointingly, my self-diagnosis of conversion disorder had not resolved my problem. Another lecture was looming. I had been asked to speak on another topic altogether at the Prado Museum in Madrid, as part of a series of talks on the old masters and modernism. The paper had been written, the PowerPoint presentation prepared. Maybe I'd go to pieces again. Maybe every time from now on I'd shake when I stood up in public. I needed help, and not from some figment of my imagination. I called a psychiatrist friend, someone I could trust to recommend a smart and serious professional. In an e-mail, he suggested that rather than hysteria, I had a version of panic disorder. What I needed was some medicine to get me through an hour at the Prado. Later, I could deal with the deeper issues that might be causing me to shake. He referred me to a pharmacologist.

Finally, I told my story to Dr. F., a real psychiatrist in a real office. He turned out to be attentive and sympathetic. He listened patiently as I described my migraine history, what I contended was a single seizure, my friend's suggestion that I had some form of panic disorder, and my own theory that I might be a conversion case. He told me frankly that my fits didn't correspond to panic disorder because I wasn't worried in advance; I had never felt I was endangered in any way, and I knew I wasn't dying. He sent me off with a prescription for six 0.5-milligram tablets of lorazepam, and a referral to an epilepsy specialist. Before I delivered my presentation in Madrid, I took the pill. I didn't shake. I made an appointment with the epilepsy specialist but canceled it.

My journey, both imagined and real, had led me in a circle, and what caused my fits was still unknown. Lorazepam probably calmed me down enough to inhibit the shaking at the Prado. It and other benzodiazepines are used to treat genuine epileptic seizures as well as panic attacks, so the effectiveness of the drug couldn't help a physician make a diagnosis in my case. On the other hand, the talk I gave had nothing to do with my father, which might have spared me the shakes in all events. And to complicate things further, a placebo might have worked just as well. It's now known that simply believing that a pill will help you can release opioids in your brain that make you feel better; or, as the authors of one study put it; "cognitive factors (e.g., expectations of pain relief) are capable of modulating physical and emotional states."[25] *Ideas*, it seems, are powerful and can alter us. As Janet pointed out, the carriage wheel doesn't have to drive over your leg; having the idea can be enough to paralyze the limb. Was it simply the idea of my father's death that made me shake? Or was it something else? The only certainty was that it wasn't available to my consciousness; I am not able to put it into words. The idea is hidden somewhere else. The question is, Is it possible to find it?

SOMETIMES THEORIES PRECEDE the technology that will prove them right, and sometimes technology races ahead of theory. The latter is true of the advances that have changed neuroscience research. PET (positron emission tomography), SPECT (single photon emission computed tomography), and fMRI (functional magnetic resonance imaging) scans have all been used to examine people's brains, as well as other organs of the body. The colored pictures that many people have seen in magazines and on television indicate blood flow to various regions of the brain. The theory is that the more oxygenated the blood flow, the more brain activity. What the pictures actually show and how to read them remains controversial, however. Time and again I have heard scientists articulate their doubts about what the images actually *mean,* and yet the pictures are often called upon as evidence, are fascinating to look at, and are useful tools despite the fact that they cannot be considered the be-all and end-all of scientific research. But when brain scans enter the popular press, they are mostly cleansed of the doubt that surrounds them. On September 26, 2006, the Science section of the *New York Times* published an article entitled "Is Hysteria Real? Brain Images Say Yes." Aside from the fact that this headline makes one wonder what is meant by the word *real,* it offers insight into misconceptions about mental illness and the mind-body relation. The unarticulated argument is that if a hysterical paralysis or seizure shows up on a brain scan, an illness once thought to be "all in your head" is actually in your body, and if it's in your body, its "reality" is confirmed. "Hysteria seemed to be a vanished 19th-century extravagance," the journalist writes, "useful for literary analysis but surely out of place in the serious reaches of contemporary science." Again, a hierarchy is established. Those pesky people who take literature seriously may have some use for hysteria, but why would scientists, the masters of culture who determine our truths, be concerned with something so retrograde as hysteria? "The word itself seems murky," she continues, "more than a little misogynistic and all too indebted to the now unfashionable Freud."[26] The journalist is right that hysteria has negative connotations for women and that even people who have never read a word of Sigmund Freud feel free to condemn his theories because his ideas, like the illness of hysteria, have fallen out of fashion. But as valuable as they may be, brain scans can't *explain* conversion.

They demonstrate that there are neuroanatomical correlates to a hysterical paralysis or blindness—an organic change—but how that happens can't be discovered from an fMRI; nor do those images tell doctors how to treat their conversion patients. As Sean Spence noted in *Advances in Psychiatric Treatment* after reviewing brain-imaging studies of conversion symptoms as well as other psychiatric disorders that involve some *body* problem, including anorexia and auditory hallucinations: "Perhaps the most chastening lesson from this review is the lack of specificity of any of the findings so far described. Although we might predict that a patient describing bodily disturbance of 'some kind' will exhibit abnormalities of certain candidate brain regions, we would have great difficulty modifying their diagnosis or treatment on the basis of brain scanning."[27] Nevertheless, the symptoms in conversion are as "real" as any other symptoms, and they may be associated with emotional shocks or traumas.

Justine Etchevery was Charcot's first hysterical patient. Before she came to the Salpêtrière, her life had been a catalog of miseries. One of fourteen children, she watched most of her siblings die young. She survived both typhoid and cholera. In an institution where she was employed, a man assaulted and tried to rape her. At twenty-five, she had her first convulsive attack, fell into a fire, and was left badly burned and blind in one eye. By the time she arrived at the Salpêtrière, she was suffering from paralysis and a lack of feeling on her left side. Once in the hospital, she had another violent seizure, lost the use of her left arm and, not long after, of all her limbs. The "contractures" lasted eight years. And then, on May 22, 1874, as she was lying in her hospital bed, she had a sudden choking fit, noticed that the stiffness in her right jaw and leg had relaxed, and cried out to the nursing sisters, "I want to get out of bed! I want to walk!" After years of paralysis, Justine climbed out of her bed and walked.[28] Hysteria can be the stuff of miracles.

The following is a brief history of another conversion patient described in an appendix to an article in *Brain* in 2001.

Patient V.U. Forty-year-old right-handed woman who fled from Algeria during childhood, escaping a shooting where relatives were killed. Chronic neck pain with left arm irradiation for several years after car accident with no injury, but no previous somatoform or psychiatry diagnosis. Left arm weakness and numbness 2 months after moving furniture when being forced to move home to Switzerland. She could not raise and maintain left arm outstretched, only slight and slow movements of her fingers. Decreased sensation to light touch on the whole arm without radicular distribution.[29]

Although the *Brain* authors draw an implicit connection between the awful events that had befallen this woman and her illness, they don't remark on them. Their job was to look at brain scans, where they found subcortical "asymmetries" in all of their seven patients, asymmetries that vanished in the four who recovered. Like Justine, V.U. suffered not one but several traumatic experiences, over which she had no control. The similarity between her childhood "escape" and her "forced" move as an adult cannot be ignored. The original event is mirrored in the later one.

The *DSM* does not tell stories. It contains no cases of actual patients or even fictional ones. Etiology, the study of the *cause* of illness, isn't part of the volume. Its mission is to be purely descriptive, to collect symptoms under headings that will help a physician diagnose patients. There is a companion *DSM-IV Casebook*, but notably, these narratives about real doctors and patients are gathered in their own volume, separate from the diagnostic tome. The fact is that all patients have stories, and those stories are necessarily part of the *meaning* of their illnesses. This may be even more true for psychiatric patients, whose stories are often so enmeshed with the sickness that one can't be untangled from the other.

One day at the hospital I worked with a fifteen-year-old girl. B. was my only student that afternoon, and I told her that I had come to do some writing with her. She said she didn't want to write. I replied that I never forced anyone to write, and we talked for a while. Then, without warning, she picked up her pencil and poured out a story about two girls.

They met in school, liked each other, and began to correspond with each other in notebooks, which they exchanged
daily. The secrecy was necessary because both girls had violent, angry fathers and were afraid that they would be over-
heard if they talked on the phone. In their daily written
communications they were able to find some solace, but
after a few months, one of the girls' fathers discovered his
daughter's notebook, and only days later, he left town with
her. The girl who remained never saw her friend again. I
praised the story and said that it was terribly sad. That was
when my student looked up and said, "It's my story." Then
she paused, looked me in the eyes, and added, "You see, I
was beaten by my father and raped by my brother. That's
why things are so hard for me." It was difficult to answer
her. When I left the hospital that day, I asked myself if it was
possible to distinguish between her illness and the story she
had told me of violence and rape. Wasn't that narrative part
of the sickness itself? Can the two be separated?

Désiré-Magloire Bourneville was a young alienist who
worked with Charcot and wrote detailed clinical accounts
of hysterical patients at the Salpêtrière. "In their delirium,"
he wrote, "hysterics have remembrances [*réminiscences*] of
long ago events in their lives, physical pains as well as psychological feelings [*des émotions morales*], events which
have set off their attacks in the past . . . nothing is more
sure than that they remember these emotional events."[30]
Later, Freud and Breuer would write these far more famous
words: "Hysterics suffer mainly from reminiscences."[31] The
girl in the hospital wasn't a conversion patient. I don't know

what her diagnosis was, but she was obviously traumatized by her memories of having been hurt and violated.
True stories can't be told forward, only backward. We invent them from the vantage point of an ever-changing present and tell ourselves how they unfolded. Why one person
who has been badly treated by a parent turns into a psy-
chopath and another with similar treatment suffers from
severe depression and yet another develops an inexplicable
paralysis isn't clear. What is clear is that memory is essential
to who we are, and memories can be both implicit and
explicit—unconscious and conscious. Freud wasn't the first
to argue that most of what the brain does is unconscious.
The nineteenth-century English physiologist William Car-
penter, the German psychologist Gustav Fechner, and the
German physicist Hermann von Helmholtz all maintained
that there was a psychological unconscious, not just a physiological one. Thoughts, memories, and ideas could reside
outside of our awareness. Freud tried to understand how
unconscious processes in the psyche work.

No neuroscientist now disputes the existence of an unconscious. But it's strange to think that not long ago, the
very idea was regarded with suspicion. After my bout in
Mount Sinai Hospital I was sent to a psychologist, Dr. E.,
who taught me biofeedback. I was hooked up to a machine
with electrodes, and over a period of eight months I learned
how to relax, how to increase my blood circulation, warm
my extremities, and reduce my pain. Dr. E. was a behaviorist. I vividly remember him saying: "If there is an unconscious, who cares?" Behaviorism closed the door on the

unconscious because its advocates asserted that everything that needed to be understood about human beings could be deduced from looking at their behavior—a third-person view. The murky regions of the first person presented a trap. And yet illness, any illness, is always experienced *by some-one*. There is a phenomenology of being sick, one that depends on temperament, personal history, and the culture in which we live.

I CONTINUED TO SHAKE. I shook even with lorazepam, but not at every public appearance, only some. When my last novel was published, the one narrated by my imaginary brother, in which I used parts of the memoir my father had written for his family and friends, and I read sections from it aloud to audiences, I shook. When I found myself on a panel in Australia discussing death in literature, I shook. The story always played out the same way. If I kept talking, the shudder would subside, but it takes great control *not* to be distracted by a violent convulsion of your own body, and I began to wonder if I could bear up. What had once taken me by surprise became familiar. What had seemed a bizarre occurrence with no conscious identifiable emotion connected to it began to look more and more like an extreme form of stage fright—entirely irrational but exclusively connected to moments when I was exposed to public scrutiny. Everything associated with performance made me anxious and distressed. At any moment, the unruly saboteur inside me might appear and disrupt the proceedings. It was then that I discovered the beta-blocker Inderal. Years ago, I'd taken Inderal for migraine. It had done no good for the headache, but on the advice of a friend I tried 10 milligrams of the drug before readings or talks, and it *worked*. Inderal (or propranolol) is a blood pressure medicine; an adrenoceptor blocker, it shuts down the release of stress hormones.

One would imagine that my narrative of the shaking woman ends here, that the successful elimination of my seizures during events in front of strangers would have filled me with relief, perhaps even joy, but that is not what has happened. While I was on a tour in Germany and Switzerland, I popped propranolol before every reading in the six cities I visited and had no tremor. In the last city, Zurich, I took the pill and read without shaking, but I felt the quiver internally throughout the event, an electric buzz running up and down my limbs. It was like shaking without shaking. While I read, I scolded myself internally, saying repeatedly, "Own this. This is you. Own it!" Of course, the fact that I spoke to myself in the second person suggests the split that had taken place—a grim sense that two Siris were present, not one. By then, I was exhausted from traveling from one city to another, from giving interviews and readings every day, from relentless anxiety about shaking, and from offering up deep parts of my inner life to others in the form of readings from a book that had come directly out of my father's death. While a pharmacological solution inhibited the outward problem, it didn't solve the mystery. It did not tell me what had happened.

Beta-blockers have been used to treat heart disease, anx-

iety, glaucoma, hyperthyroidism, and neurological problems such as migraine. In *Basic and Clinical Pharmacology*,
under a section titled "Neurologic Diseases," the authors
admit that they do not know why propranolol is sometimes
effective for migraine. They go on to say, "Since sympathetic
activity may enhance skeletal muscle tremor, it is not surprising that *beta antagonists have been found to reduce certain tremors.* The somatic manifestations of anxiety may
respond dramatically to low doses of propranolol especially
when taken prophylactically. For example, benefit has been
found in musicians with performance anxiety ('stage
fright')."[32] (My italics.) "Sympathetic activity" is a part of
the autonomic nervous system, the part of us that goes into
high gear during an emergency or a stressful situation. It is
automatic and involuntary. All this fits my case, but why did
I, without any warning, suddenly come down with stage
fright when I was fifty-one years old? For some reason, after
many years of relative calm, I developed not just the easily
hidden, nervous tremor I had experienced before, but huge,
near-toppling spasms. And why didn't I feel anxiety before
my first bout of shakes if it was related to anxiety? Why can
I speak calmly through every seizure? Where is the heart-
thumping, breathless feeling of panic I have experienced in
other situations?

PROPRANOLOL IS ALSO USED to treat the repetitive debilitating memories of post-traumatic stress disorder. It doesn't
eliminate the memories; rather, it decreases their intensity
and makes them more bearable. The cognitive scientist Larry

Cahill conducted a research study that demonstrated the effects of the drug on memory. Two groups of people were shown a series of slides that in the beginning were identical. Everyone saw the same first four slides, but then the narrative diverged into either a neutral story (a boy and his parents visit a hospital and watch emergency drill procedures) or an emotionally arousing story (the boy is badly injured in an accident and is rushed to the hospital, where the surgeons reattach his severed feet).[33] Before watching one of the two stories, subjects were given either propranolol or a placebo. Two weeks later, the participants were told to return, but they were not informed that their memories for the slides would be tested. The results showed that subjects who had taken the placebo had enhanced memory for the accident story, but those who took propranolol did not. People tested about the same for the neutral slides. When we have strong emotional experiences, the stress hormones epinephrine (adrenaline) and cortisol are released in our brains and appear to act as stimuli for keeping memories alive. Propranolol, however, interferes with the release of those hormones and blocks the effect emotional excitement has on recollection. It seems, however, to have no influence on people's ordinary or more neutral memories.[34]

Emotional memories also appear to be processed and stored differently in the brain from more pedestrian memories, which may explain the phenomenon of traumatic flashbacks. A neurobiological study conducted in 1996 on people who experienced flashbacks concluded that these memories are "organized on a perceptual and affective level with limited semantic representation and tend to intrude as emotional or sensory fragments related to the original event, with stability over time."[35] This is an elaborate way of saying that what returns in a flashback is remembered not through language but through emotion and sensation. After a car accident, I had flashbacks four nights in a row. Each time I was asleep, and each time I woke sitting up in bed, terrified, my heart racing, after reliving the moment of the crash: the speeding van, the deafening noise of glass and metal exploding around me. For four nights in a row, I relived the shock of that van as it slammed into the passenger side of the car, where I was sitting. These were not like any memories I have ever had. I had not sought them, and they had not been triggered by some external stimulus—a smell or taste or sight or sound. They just came, and when they came, they were not in the past but in the present. The thing that had happened, happened again.

IN *HISTORY BEYOND TRAUMA*, Françoise Davoine and Jean-Max Gaudillière, two psychoanalysts who have done extensive work in the field, address this curious alteration of time among those who have been traumatized. " 'Once upon a time,' " they write, "becomes 'Once upon no time.' "[36] Trauma memory has no narration. Stories always take place in *time*. They have a sequence, and they are always behind us. Those four nights of reenactment were wordless. I could not say, *Oh, yes, that happened four days ago when my husband, daughter, our dog, and I were driving home from the country. A speeding van hit us at an intersection. The car was completely destroyed, but we all survived.* The experience had no context (returning from the country), no place (where Third Street and Fourth Avenue in Brooklyn cross), and was in no way diminished by distance (it isn't happening now; it happened yesterday or the day before or the day before that). The violence burst into my sleep from nowhere and shocked me with the same force as the accident itself.

I know the impact was horrible, because it returned to me those four nights, but my memory of the catastrophic instant is no longer present in my mind. I remember the time *after* the crash, however, with heightened clarity and precision. I remember sitting frozen in the seat, remember checking to see that I was whole without moving my head. I remember looking through the shattered glass of the windshield at the sky and that everything was black and white and gray. I remember the fireman telling me that the Jaws of Life were noisy, and I remember my indifference, an indifference so profound that I actually said to myself, If you have to die now, this is not such a bad way to go. In the ambulance, the paramedic who was monitoring my swiftly dropping blood pressure as the siren screamed above us asked me if I was particularly white. I told him that because I was of northern European stock, I was indeed white, but that people did not often comment on my whiteness. No doubt, after the accident, I had turned very pale. I didn't know then whether or not I had broken my neck, whether or not I would die or be injured for life, but I felt neither fear nor distress. My perceptions were acute. In fact, I told myself to be alert to everything because if I did get through it, I might be able to use the material in a novel. Under the circumstances, this now strikes me as bizarre, but my distance from potential catastrophe must have served a protective, adaptive purpose: alienation as armor against the real. The little voice in my head continued on its narrative journey, talking away in a reasonable manner, but my emotions had shut down.

In their book *The Haunted Self,* Onno van der Hart, Ellert R. S. Nijenhuis, and Kathy Steele discuss trauma and dissociation.[37] Following Janet and others, they argue that dissociative experiences are due to a division in psychobiological systems within the suffering person. Using terminology developed by Charles Myers, who studied trauma, especially among veterans of the First World War, they use Apparently Normal Personality and Emotional Personality to identify the split, or ANP and EP. Although this distinction can become unintentionally comic—her ANP did this, while her EP did that—the terms make some sense to me. The danger is that this language reduces a complex reality to something far too simple, even though the authors who use it want to maintain a sense of the intricate mechanisms involved. ANP and EP move dangerously close to multiple personality, a diagnosis that has made many people uneasy because, for a time, psychotherapists seemed to be finding multiples all over the place. Hosts and alters were everywhere, as were recovered traumatic memories, some of them highly suspicious. The *DSM*'s response was to change multiple personality disorder to dissociative identity disorder, or DID. This deemphasizes the many-people-inside-one-person quality of the illness and stresses that there is something wrong with the patient's whole *identity*. Rather than being several discrete persons, the multiple is a being in pieces. As Ian Hacking points out in *Rewriting the Soul: Multiple Personality and the Sciences of Memory,* perception changes illness: "Some physicians had multiples among their patients in the 1840s, but their picture of the disorder was very different from the one that is common in the 1990s. The doctors' vision was different because the patients were different; but the patients were different because the doctors' expectations were different."[38] In other words, suggestion is powerful, and human beings are far more vulnerable to it than we would like to imagine.

Hacking doesn't argue that there aren't traumatized people or that they don't suffer from what can sometimes be odd symptoms. He tracks the historical development of a diagnosis that was popular in the nineteenth century and, significantly, regarded as a form of *hysteria*. Multiple personality receded along with hysteria and then rose again in the late twentieth century in a different form. Hacking dislikes the word *dissociation* because its meaning is broad and it is used to refer to a number of states. I think his objection is deepened by the fact that the word itself became a banner for the defenders of multiple personality disorder during the 1990s when wars over recovered memory were raging and psychotherapists published papers in journals called *Dissociation* and the *International Society for the Study of Dissociation*. He is right that the word has become diffuse and has been employed by doctors who may have prompted plurality in their patients through suggestion. Nevertheless, there does seem to be a defensive response in human beings that involves some form of distancing from or translation of the unbearable—proximity to one's own death or to the deaths of others. Justine in 1874 and V.U. in 2001 inhabited different medical climates, but that doesn't mean we can't see similarities between them.

The strangeness of a duality in myself remains, a powerful sense of an "I" and an uncontrollable other. The shaking woman is certainly not anyone with a *name*. She is a speechless alien who appears only during my speeches. At one of his Harvard lectures, Janet referred to a case of hysterical trembling. "In some rare cases, you can find behind the tremors . . . the existence of a fixed idea separated from the consciousness. . . . But, in most cases, there is nothing behind the tremor but a *vague emotive state* and a kind of transformation of the motor function of the limbs."[39] When addressing cases of hysterical anesthesia, he wrote, "In reality what has disappeared is not the elementary sensation . . . it is the faculty that enables the subject to say clearly, 'It is I who feel, it is I who hear.' "[40] Hysteria, from this point of view, is a derangement of subjectivity, of ownership of the self.

But who owns the self? Is it the "I"? What does it mean to be integrated and not in pieces? What is subjectivity? Is it a singular property or a plural one? I have come to think of the shaking woman as an untamed other self, a Mr. Hyde to my Dr. Jekyll, a kind of double. Doubles in literature almost always torment and sabotage the desires and ambitions of their originals and, often, they take over. Poe's uncanny twin and rival in "William Wilson" is identical to the first William Wilson in every way except that he cannot speak above a whisper, a haunting echo of the narrator's own voice. Dostoyevsky's benighted hero in *The Double,* Mr. Golyadkin, shakes in his doctor's office shortly before the crafty, ambitious second Mr. Golyadkin makes his appearance: "His gray eyes gleamed strangely, his lips began to quiver, all the muscles, all the features of his face began moving and working. He was trembling all over."[41] In Hans Christian Andersen's story "The Shadow," it is a shadow that subsumes its owner: "For now the shadow was master and the master shadow."[42] Original and copy are at war.

But doubling stories also exist outside fiction in the neurological literature. Some migraine sufferers have seen doubles of themselves as part of their auras. Known as autoscopic hallucinations, these visions are mirrors of the self. The migraineur sees her double, sometimes motionless, but often walking beside her and copying her every gesture. The neurologist Klaus Podoll, who has done extensive research on migraine auras, includes on the website he shares with his colleague Markus Dahlem a story about the Swedish botanist Carolus Linnaeus, who often saw his double before a migraine attack and once is reported to have entered a lecture hall to speak, noticed there was already someone at the lectern, and left the room. He had mistaken his own hallucinatory double for someone else.[43] In a paper, Todd Feinberg and Raymond Shapiro tell the story of a patient, S.M., who had atrophy in the right temporoparietal region of her brain. S.M. mistook her own mirror image for a double, whom she referred to as the "other S.M." Because S.M. was deaf, she used sign language to communicate with her mirror image. S.M. got along rather well with her second self, but she confessed to a few discrepancies between them. The other S.M. wasn't as proficient at signing and wasn't as bright as S.M. herself.[44] If I were fated to see myself from the outside as another, without the ability to identify that person as myself, heaven knows what flaws I might detect. In contrast to S.M., another patient of Feinberg's, Rosamund, detested her mirror image and, like William Wilson, treated it as an evil twin: "You tramp! Go on home . . . leave us alone!"[45] Her fury mounted until she threatened to kill the intruder. At the very least these stories indicate that any conception of the self as unitary might be subject to revision. S.M. and Rosamund misread only their own images in the mirror, not the reflections of others, which suggests that there is something neurologically distinct about the reflective recognition of one's self. The two women easily recognized the reflections of others in the mirror and, had either of their doctors pointed to his patient's body and asked her to identify to whom it belonged, neither woman would have had any difficulty claiming it as her own.

Infants and most animals do not recognize themselves in mirrors. My dog Jack had no interest in his own reflection and had no idea that it belonged to him. At some moment in their development, human beings, some primates, elephants, and a species of dolphin are able to know they are looking not at others but at themselves. It is a privilege of the highly evolved. The psychoanalyst Jacques Lacan named this turn in human life the mirror stage (*stade de miroir*), identifying the moment when a child looks at her own reflection and sees herself as an externalized whole, as if she were gazing at herself through the eyes of another person.[46] But most of the time we do not see ourselves whole. I see only parts of my body, my hands and part of my arm when I type, for example, or none of it when I stroll through the street taking in the sights and sounds and smells. In his essay "The Child's Relation to Others," Maurice Merleau-Ponty writes, "The consciousness I have of my own body is not the consciousness of an isolated mass; it is a postural schema [*schéma corporel*]."[47] It is an *introceptive* sense, to borrow the philosopher's vocabulary. Following Merleau-Ponty, Shaun Gallagher proposes making a distinction between *body schema* and *body image*. The former is "a system of sensory motor capacities,"[48] a mostly unconscious system. When I reach for a glass, I don't have to watch my arm reach for it or measure the distance between my hand and the glass; I do it without thinking.

My body image, on the other hand, is conscious—the beliefs and thoughts I have about my physical being. I'm fat or thin or ugly or beautiful; it is I as an object, a perception of my body from the *outside*, and I would suggest what Gallagher doesn't dwell on, that an important part of that construction takes place linguistically. But there is a deeply emotional quality to self-recognition as well. Seeing the self has a particular affective resonance, and if that familiar feeling doesn't happen, the reflection loses its meaning. S.M. had retained good operation of her body schema but could be said to have lost one aspect of her body image, the ability to say, *That's not another person, that's myself standing there in the mirror.* She, too, suffered a lapse in subjectivity, a failure of one aspect of her self-ownership—in this case, ownership of her reflection.

Human beings are binary creatures: two arms, two legs, two eyes, two ears, two nostrils, and two hemispheres of the brain that look alike, although the two sides are said to be dominant for different functions. They communicate with each other through the neural fibers that attach the two halves, the corpus callosum. In the 1960s, Roger Sperry began his experiments on patients who, due to intractable epileptic seizures, had undergone an operation called a commissurotomy: their corpus collosums had been severed. "Each disconnected hemisphere," Sperry said in his Nobel Prize acceptance speech, "behaved as if it were not conscious of the cognitive events in the partner hemisphere. . . . Each brain half, in other words, appeared to have its own, largely separate cognitive domain with its own private *perceptual* learning and memory experiences."[49] Are we two or one?

Among the stranger stories in neurology are those of people who appear to be torn in half. Their doubles take up residence in their own bodies, and their right and left sides do battle. When the right hand buttons up a shirt, the left hand unbuttons it. When the right hand opens a drawer, the left slams it shut. After their surgeries, some split-brain patients developed "strange" or "alien hand" syndrome. Dahlia Zaidel recorded some of their comments: "My left hand takes my cigarette out of my mouth while I'm smoking"; "I turn on the water with my right hand and the left turns it off."[50] People with a hand that rebels often berate the offending limb, crying out, "Bad hand!" or slapping it to restrain it from making further mischief. One man had to subdue a hand that had a marked tendency to creep up his thigh and head for his genitals, even when there were other people in the room. In 1908, the German neurologist Kurt Goldstein reported a case of a woman with a demon hand: "On one occasion, the hand grabbed her own neck and tried to throttle her and could only be pulled off by force."[51] After the woman's death, the physician discovered multiple lesions in her brain, including one in the corpus callosum. None of these people would identify the impetuous, conniving hand as "I." Indeed, in these cases, the offending limb seems to have an insurrectionist life of its own and is identified in the third person as outside the self, a force entirely opposed to the will of its owner. Usually, although not always, it's the *left* hand that is delinquent. The motor functions of the left hand are controlled by the right hemisphere of the brain, just as the left hemisphere controls the right hand. The areas that control the "I," the first-person subject who speaks, however, usually reside in the left hemisphere, in the language areas of the brain, the sites Freud discussed in his book on aphasia. In alien hand syndrome there is a well-functioning "I," a law-abiding, thinking, speaking self that is conscious and has civilized intentions, and another *thing* or *it* that seems to be operating without permission.

I am the one who hears. It is I who feels and thinks and sees and speaks. This is where I begin and where I end. I identify myself in the mirror. I see you. You are looking at me. This is my narrating self, my conscious, telling self. But it is *not* the shaking self, nor the flashback self. Mark Solms and Oliver Turnbull cite one of Sperry's experiments on a split-brain patient in their book *The Brain and the Inner World*. An image is briefly flashed on a screen. In such patients, the right hemisphere will perceive the image, but it won't be accessible to the left. A woman was shown pornographic pictures. She giggled but couldn't explain her reaction. "This case," the authors write, "demonstrates that an entire cerebral hemisphere can process information unconsciously." More importantly, they argue, "For someone to reflect consciously on visual experience, he or she has to re-code the visual experiences into words."[52] Language appears to be vital to self-reflexive awareness, the ability to say, *I saw sexy pictures on the screen that embarrassed and titillated me,* but it is not necessary for registering the images and responding to them. Versions of this right/left brain division have led to popular but simplistic notions of right- and left-brain personalities and other reductive speculations, such as attributing consciousness to the left hemisphere and unconsciousness to the right. Sperry and others have shown that the right brain isn't entirely aphasic or nonverbal, although it is regarded as dominant for spatial and imagistic functions.

Some patients who can't say why they feel shocked, amused, or frightened by an unconscious perception *confabulate*. S.M. saw her reflection, didn't recognize it, couldn't *feel* it was herself, and so she confabulated another S.M.

Confabulation isn't lying; the neurological term refers to the explanations brain-damaged people come up with to explain the mysteries that confront them. When the right hemisphere takes in a picture and the information isn't sent to the left, the verbal neocortex will do its best to explain what's going on. Michael Gazzaniga, who worked with split-brain patients, called this "the left brain interpreter."[53] Those of us with intact corpus callosums have more fluid correspondence between the hemispheres of our brain, but we, too, interpret the mysteries of various stimuli, internal or external, that come our way. The shaking woman is not the narrating woman. The narrating, interpreting woman continued on while the other shook. The narrator was a fluent generator of sentences and explanations. It is she who is writing now. I confess that in my gloomier moments I have wondered if a whole host of intellectual theories don't fall into the category of grand confabulations.

Again, it's important to note that not *all* split-brain patients have hands with lives of their own, only some. Even when people have similar lesions or commissuritomies, the damage or cut cannot infallibly predict symptoms, which means that a purely anatomical investigation will not provide an answer to why this happens. What is, in fact, most remarkable about split-brain people isn't their deficits but how few problems they seem to have. Of course, these surgeries do not cut the entire nervous system in half. The brain stem is not severed, so some communication remains between the two sides. Brains are also plastic and adaptive to changed circumstances. Younger brains are more malleable than old ones. An infant who loses an entire hemisphere of his brain can grow up to be astonishingly normal. A child who loses his sight early is far more adaptable than an adult who goes blind; the areas of the brain devoted to vision will be remapped for the other senses, especially auditory functions. Brains can reroute themselves, and it now appears that although plasticity decreases as we grow older, it never stops. All the split-brain patients studied retained a strong sense of an "I" and a working left-brain interpreter, even when that interpreter was wrong about what had been seen by the right hemisphere. Their linguistic functions worked perfectly.

"I" exists only in relation to "you." Language takes place *between* people, and it is acquired through others, even though we have the biological equipment necessary to learn it. If you lock a child in a closet, he will not learn to speak. Language is outside us and inside us, part of a complex dialectical reality between people. Words cross the borders of our bodies in two directions, outside in and inside out, and therefore the minimal requirement for a living language is two people. The first time I encountered a language for two was in a pair of identical twins in my hometown. The girls were about three when their parents noticed that they communicated in a dialect all their own. F. and T. grew up in a bilingual family—French and English—and seemed to have looted bits and pieces of both languages to create a peculiar hybrid of their own. In the 1930s, the Russian neurologists A. R. Luria and F. Yudovich did a study on two brothers, six-year-old identical twins who, like F. and T., had developed their own language, based on gestures and some primitive nouns. The boys showed significant cognitive and developmental delays in every area. The neurologists separated the twins and, in rather brutal Soviet style, decided to give language lessons to only one of them: Twin A, the underling of the duo. Twin A quickly outstripped his brother, Twin B, in language skills. He began to speak in sentences with verb tenses and syntax, and he developed an imagination—that is, he was able to project himself into the future and remember himself in the past. He also gained the ability to understand nonverbal games that had eluded him earlier. Before he acquired the necessary linguistic tools, he couldn't understand formal games, didn't know what to do with balls thrown to him or where to run or jump. Learning Russian ordered his mind in an entirely new way.[54] Luria did not articulate this as I would, but human *time*, essential to working consciousness and, of course, storytelling, may well arrive through language.

After an infant's birth, the brain's prefrontal cortex develops enormously in two big spurts around the ages of two and five, and it develops in relation to our experiences with others. Its neurobiology is dependent on what happens beyond it, on the vital exchanges between child and parents. The twins invented their own primitive language, which by its very character interfered with their growing up. Its lack of richness and flexibility—verb tenses in particular—created a world of an ongoing present, the sort of world in which, I suppose, my dog lived. He certainly had a memory that was alerted by cues, even a couple of linguistic ones:

walk and his own name, *Jack*. He could learn all kinds of things—to sit, to pee outside, not to jump up and eat the food on our plates—but I feel confident that he didn't day-dream about the future or long for the past. This is a human capacity that allows for an idea of time as we feel it. It lets us locate events in our lives behind us or in some imagined time ahead. But not all human experiences exist in that autobiographical sequence. If we return to Davoine and Gaudillière, their work with people who have been trauma-tized, and their declaration that "the past is the present," it's possible to understand trauma as a form of speechlessness that is located in an ongoing present. Indeed, they argue that trauma victims live "outside of time."[55] My brief flash-back experience is a testament to that fact. It was nonverbal, involuntary, and it was *not* in the past. It was happening again. The directing, thinking "I" had no part in it. Similarly, my shuddering body felt out of my control, but after a while I seemed able to wait it out, to watch as my rattling limbs slowly calmed themselves. Obviously, there is a disconnec-tion here, one we would have to call psychobiological. The propranolol served to shut the door on the rush that rises up in me through a trigger—death, my father, audience. But did my inner speech, my battle to control the shakes and re-main calm, help me subdue them before the propranolol came to the rescue?

Luria argues that speech facilitates "the transition from sensation to thinking, and to the creation of new functional systems. Speech not only gives names to the objects of the outside world; it also distinguishes among their essential properties and includes them in a system of relations to other objects. As a result, man can evoke an image of a particular object and use it in the absence of the original."[56] Freud's famous *fort/da* story of his grandson in *Beyond the Pleasure Principle* illustrates this point. The little boy played a game of disappearance and return with a wooden reel attached to a piece of string. He would throw it, saying *fort*, gone, and bring it back, joyfully saying *da*, there. Freud interpreted the game as a way for the child to master absence and presence, his mother's comings and goings.[57] Lacan later emphasized the linguistic or symbolic aspect of the game, words being used to control what is missing. We use symbols, and those symbols give us power over what is no longer there or is yet to come. We organize the past as explicit autobiographical memory, what Antonio Damasio has called "the autobiographical self"; fragments are linked in a narrative, which in turn shapes our expectations for the future. There can be no autobiographical self without language.

It was Bertha Pappenheim, Breuer's famous hysterical patient known as Anna O., who coined the English term "the talking cure." For a while she seemed to lose her ability to speak in her mother tongue and lapsed into English. Pappenheim had "an army of hysterical symptoms": coughing, paralysis, anesthesia, and contractures. She also suffered from what Charcot, Janet, and Freud and Breuer called "double consciousness"; she experienced two selves, one "psychically quite normal," according to Breuer, and another, which she referred to as her "bad self." Even while she was very ill, he states, "a keen and quiet observer was, as the patient put it, sitting in some corner of her mind, watching all the mad things go on."[58] The interpreter was present. It just wasn't able to rein in the demon.

Breuer notes that his patient's hysterical cough first began when she was sitting near her beloved father's deathbed and she heard dance music coming from a nearby house. The music triggered a desire to be with the revelers, and after that, every time she heard music "with a strong rhythm," she reacted with a "*tussis nervosa*."[59] Was the doctor right? Did music trigger an implicit memory of Pappenheim's dying father and her guilt for having wanted to leave him and join the other young people who were free to dance into the night? Can we ever really know? Can talking free a person from symptoms? When I stood in front of that tree, I glanced down at the little plaque on the ground in front of it and read my father's birth and death dates. Was that my music?

In *The Ego and the Id* (1923) Freud writes, "The question 'How does a thing become conscious?' would thus more advantageously be stated, 'How does a thing become pre-conscious [available to consciousness]?' And the answer would be 'through becoming connected to the word presentations corresponding to it.'" Further, he says, these words are "residues of memory." He does not deny that visual imagery is part of the remembered mental world, but he argues that it has another character, that being conscious of an optical memory is more concrete and that "the relations between the various elements of the subject matter, which especially characterizes thought, cannot be given visual expression. Thinking in pictures is, therefore, only a very incomplete form of becoming conscious. In some way, too, it stands nearer to unconscious processes than does thinking in words, and it is unquestionably older, both ontogenetically and phylogenetically."[60] It is striking how well Freud's distinction between the visuospatial and the audioverbal tallies with research gleaned from split-brain patients. Luria's study also illuminates the difference between the visual and the verbal. Through his language lessons, Twin A gained the thought mobility that comes with the remembered word presentations Freud described, while Twin B remained locked inside the far more concrete, noun-based language he shared with his brother, which hampered the development of his mind.

Some memories can easily be brought to consciousness. Others have grown vague or appear only in fragments. I remember a gesture—putting my glasses down on a table, but which table? Sometimes I walk downstairs to get those same reading glasses, but by the time I arrive at my destination, countless other thoughts have intervened, and I have forgotten what I wanted. Only after I've retraced my steps—climbed to the second floor again and returned to where I came from—can I remember what my mission was. The memory returns only when I repeat the movement. Once, I was looking at a crack in my coffee cup and it triggered a memory of another flaw in some other vessel I felt sure I had seen recently. I couldn't say what I was remembering—a conversation, a painting, a passage in a book—and then, all at once, I recognized that the image came from a dream, the rest of which had vanished entirely. Not long ago, my friend H. reminded me of an unpleasant but not traumatic experience I had many years ago while the two of us, then eighteen, were traveling in Europe. We found ourselves at a party. I was talking to a young man in one of the rooms of the apartment when, without warning, he threw himself at me. I fought him off, and H. and I fled. I had not thought about this brief mauling for years, and even now the memory is fractured and incoherent—a dim recollection of struggle, fear, and relief. The truth is, I don't really like remembering this particular event. It was completely outside my awareness until H. revived it. What Freud called *repression* involves memories that remain unconscious because the patient doesn't want to know about them but that then can be brought back to consciousness through the analytic process, the talking cure, which allows the speaking subject, the I, to reown the experience.

Scientists distinguish among semantic, procedural, and episodic memories. Semantic memory includes much that I know about the world, from the fact that glass will break to how skunks smell to Kierkegaard's ideas about the aesthetic. Procedural memory is implicit. I get on my bicycle and go because my body has learned how to ride it and thinking is no longer necessary. This corresponds to Merleau-Ponty's *schéma corporel* and Gallagher's *body schema*. Episodic memory, on the other hand, is explicit. It is owned by a self-conscious "I." It is literally re-collection, the act of bringing bits of the past into present consciousness. Much of this takes linguistic form, is self-reflective, and therefore makes it possible for me to see myself in myself but also to regard myself as if from afar—as someone else might see me. It allows me to speculate as David Copperfield does in the first sentence of the Charles Dickens novel that bears his name: "Whether I shall turn out to be the hero of my own life, or whether that station will be held by anybody else, these pages must show."[61]

In my writing work with psychiatric patients, I have often used a book by the poet and visual artist Joe Brainard called *I Remember*. This slim but extraordinary volume is a catalog of the author's memories. Every entry begins with the words "I remember":

I remember that I never cried in front of other people.

I remember how embarrassed I was when other children cried.

I remember the first art award I ever won. In grade school. It was a painting of a nativity scene. I remember a very large star in the sky. It won a blue ribbon at the fair.

I remember when I started smoking I wrote my parents a letter and told them so. The letter was never mentioned and I continued to smoke.[62]

When the patients and I write our own "I remembers", something remarkable happens. The very act of inscribing the words *I remember* generates memories, usually highly specific images or events from the past, often ones we hadn't thought about for many years. Writing the words *I remember* engages both motor and cognitive action. Usually I do not know how I will finish the sentence when I begin it, but once the word *remember* is on the page, some thought appears to me. One memory often leads to another. An associative chain is engaged:

I remember when I thought I had ugly knees.

I remember the man who told me my knees were beautiful.

I remember that after that, I never thought they were ugly again.

My hand moves to write, a procedural bodily memory of unconscious knowing, which evokes a vague feeling or sense of some past image or event emerging into consciousness. Then the episodic memory is present and can be articulated with startling suddenness. No matter how minute, comic, or sad their memories may be, the writers in my class inevitably find pleasure in extracting small nuggets from their mental gold mines. The most vivid memories emerge, seemingly from nowhere. There is no given theme. All memories are welcome. After this exercise, many of my students have left the class astonished. "I haven't thought about that for years," they say or "I had forgotten all about

Uncle Fred's three-legged cat until just now." Because emotion consolidates memory, the reminiscences are rarely neutral—they are often rich in the subtleties of feeling. The written incantation *I remember* is vital as a catalyst. It assumes ownership of what is to come. This is mine, and even though it is difficult to explain how these recollections emerge from hidden depths into the light of day, once they have arrived, they belong to the writer, and for a psychiatric patient being treated in a hospital, for a person who is often overwhelmed by an illness that makes it difficult to integrate the various pieces of himself, who feels he is falling apart, the words *I remember* are in themselves therapeutic. They seem to initiate a brief, coherent inscribed memory. Joe Brainard discovered a memory machine.

Writing *I remember* appears to function differently from just saying the words *I remember*. I was intrigued to come across the case of a thirteen-year-old boy, identified by the pseudonym Neil, in a paper published in *Brain* in 1994. After being treated with radiation for an invasive brain tumor, Neil continued to speak fluently, but his reading ability gradually deteriorated over a period of two years, until his alexia was total; he could not read at all. He developed vision problems, had trouble naming familiar objects and identifying faces, and although he had a detailed memory of his life before his tumor and the treatment, he was unable to recall his life afterward. When one of the researchers queried him about his everyday memory failures, Neil said, "If I ask the teacher a question, by the time she has answered me, I have forgotten what I have asked." The boy could, however, make elaborate, careful drawings of things and scenes, some of which were reproduced in the article—a Christmas tree, a rabbit in a yard, a juice bottle and a corkscrew—even though he couldn't identify them. It eventually became clear that while Neil had no memory of his world that he could *talk* about, he could remember what had happened to him when he *wrote* it down, despite the fact that he was unable to recall or read back what he had written. His memory appeared to exist solely in a mind-hand motor connection. For example, in response to his mother's question about what he had done in school that day, he wrote for her, "Today in school I watched the film my left foot (My Left Foot). I also had geography. I saw [name of the teacher] and he was very pleased. Miss [name of the teacher] is going to give us a note about activities in the holidays." When his mother asked him if he had enjoyed seeing the film, he said, "What film?" The authors of the paper also noted that, through writing, Neil was better able to recover meaningful memories—his experiences with friends and family—than the neutral lists of words that the researchers would test him on. Neil's postmorbid, exclusively orthographic memory was enhanced by emotion, just as it is for the rest of us who have normal recall for events. My hand moves as I write the words *I remember,* and the act itself seems to initiate recollections. As he traced the letters onto a page, Neil was able to inscribe what the rest of him had forgotten. The talking Neil had amnesia. Neil's writing hand did not.[63]

The *Brain* authors do not know what to make of Neil's

SIRI HUSTVEDT

case. They do say that his "performance" resembles "automatic writing, a dissociative phenomenon that was once the subject of intensive study in both experimental and clinical psychology."⁶⁴ They do not say that automatic writing was viewed as both a spontaneous symptom of and used as a therapy for hysteria. Janet employed the technique with hypnotized patients to bring out traumatic narratives that had split off from their conscious minds. His theory was that these patients were not capable of integrating the sensory material that had bombarded them, which then resulted in a dissociation of their sensorimotor processes. When he suggested that they write under hypnosis, the narratives they spontaneously produced helped make them aware of what had gone underground. Neil's brain damage created a split—his consciousness did not include what his writing hand appeared to remember. The authors also mention a 1986 study of two "neuropsychiatric patients" with temporal lobe epilepsy and an affective disorder who produced pages of text without knowing it. Surely these phenomena are related. The question is, How? And why do the researchers, who seem aware of the earlier medical history, resist discussing it?

Automatic writing was widely studied in the late nineteenth and early twentieth centuries. In his book *Psychopathology of Hysteria* published in 1913, Charles D. Fox describes the phenomenon (in prose that reminds us jargon is nothing new to medicine):

In order that automatic writing can occur there must be a coexistent dissociation of consciousness with elimination of the automatically functionating extremity from the field of consciousness. Not only are the motor functions dissociated but, commonly, the member as a whole is elided from consciousness with the result that sensory impressions originating in the part are not consciously perceived.[65]

Although the authors of the *Brain* paper claim that Neil's case has no precedent, which may be true, there is a related and famous case: A. R. Luria's patient Zazetsky, whom the neurologist chronicled in his book *The Man with a Shattered World*. After a severe injury in the Second World War, in which the left parieto-occipital areas of his brain were damaged, Zazetsky found himself with grave spatial and cognitive deficits. Like Neil, he could speak and repeat words, but he couldn't remember his name or address or the words for the things around him. He sagely identified what had disappeared as his "speech memory." After a couple of months in the hospital, he slowly began to recall fragments of his past, his name, mailing address, and more words:

I heard everything people around me were saying, and little by little my head was crammed with songs, stories, and bits of conversations I'd picked up. As I began to remember words and use them in thinking, my vocabulary became more flexible.

At first I couldn't remember any of the words I wanted to use in a letter. But I finally decided to write home and quickly got off a letter—a short one, just a note. *I was completely unable to read what I'd written* and somehow didn't want to show it to any of the patients. In order not to think about it and risk getting upset, I quickly sealed the envelope with my family's address on it and sent it off to be mailed. [My italics.]⁶⁶

Zazetsky would always have terrible problems reading and understanding what he had written, but he could write and when he wrote he remembered, especially if he didn't lift his writing hand from the page. In his voluminous notebooks, Zazetsky not only described the hardships caused by his ravaged brain, he also painstakingly brought back every memory he could extract from his scattered mind. Despite his disabilities, he was a man who retained a supreme sense of self-conscious awareness, a labile, thinking "I." The extracts from Zazetsky's notebooks reveal a person of remarkable character. Intellectually curious, analytical, and emotionally sensitive, Zazetsky bears decisive witness to the strange and distinct power of writing as a memory tool.

I OFTEN WONDER HOW much I've forgotten. Perhaps daily "I remember" exercises would help me recover lost pieces of my life. Neil seemed to have a memory system that was encoding and storing all kinds of daily memories in a "place" completely separate from his ordinary waking consciousness, which was badly impaired. Don't reading and writing go together? In both Neil and Zazetsky, these seemingly related functions separated: one vanished; the other stayed.

Do I shake because I have a systemic disconnection? A couple of times since the advent of propranolol in my life, the tremor has surprised me again. As I sat down to do a television interview for a Swedish program, I felt the buzz rise in my limbs. It had not occurred to me that I should have taken pills in anticipation. This was a small, relaxed affair— an interviewer and cameraman. They had set up in the back room of a restaurant. I felt tranquil until that tuning fork began to hum. I gripped the arms of the chair hard, praying it wouldn't erupt into seizure-like spasms. It didn't, but the fact that it didn't seemed arbitrary, the whim of an unknown stranger. Another time, I was shocked to feel the first hint of the shudder when I was in my own house. I opened my mouth to read a small piece I had written for a young man who was gathering short stories about Berlin for a radio program. I excused myself and ran for the medicine cabinet.

Who are we, anyway? What do I actually know about myself? My symptom has taken me from the Greeks to the present day, in and out of theories and thoughts that are built on various ways of seeing the world. What is body and what is mind? Is each of us a singular being or a plural one? How do we remember things and how do we forget them? Tracking my pathology turns out to be an adventure in the history of experience and perception. How do we *read* a symptom or an illness? How do we frame what we observe? What is inside the frame and what falls outside it? Janet's patients didn't have brain scans, but Neil did. Neil's scan does not explain his dissociated orthographic memory.

Automatic writing once had a place in medical theory. Now it is an outcast, a curiosity that stuns researchers. Why?

Although interest in Janet has grown a little recently, most of his works have been out of print for years. From a historical point of view, a large part of the reason is hypnosis. When hypnosis was discredited in the late nineteenth century, the reputations of Charcot, Janet, and others who had used it on their patients were badly damaged. This is ironic because Charcot had rescued hypnotism from its association with the Austrian doctor Franz Anton Mesmer. Mesmer's idea of cure by animal magnetism had caused a stir a century before Charcot, but his science was later soundly rejected by the medical establishment. Charcot revived the practice of hypnotism at the Salpêtrière, only to have his use of it damage his legacy. One of Charcot's mistakes was to maintain that *only* hysterics could be hypnotized, a conviction that turned out to be false. As the Swedish physician Axel Munthe commented at the time, "If the statement of the Salpêtrière school that only hysterical subjects were hypnotizable was correct it would mean that at least eighty-five percent of mankind was suffering from hysteria."[67] The fact that Charcot staged elaborate public spectacles of hypnotized patients performing their illnesses for audiences also hurt him. He had a tendency to treat his patients as if they were props to demonstrate his theories. And, as Georges Didi-Huberman argues in his book *Invention of Hysteria*, Charcot's use of photography as an "objective" tool to record the illness was rife with sexual bias and manipulations that created a vision of hysteria as fundamentally theatrical, an idea that has never left us.[68] In ordinary parlance, *hysteria* still means dramatic emotional display. Early in his career, Freud hypnotized his patients and offered them suggestions, but he later admitted that he wasn't good at it and stopped. He also found it convenient to distance himself from the French school, which had come under a barrage of criticism. Worries about the power of a doctor's suggestions to influence and shape his patient's mind, whether they are made under hypnosis or not, are still with us. The fear has haunted psychoanalysis, psychotherapy, and many forms of psychiatric treatment since Charcot. The bitter battles fought over memory, "recovered" and/or "false," are a continuation of this very same dispute, albeit using different language.

Nevertheless, in popular consciousness, *hysteria* and *automatic writing* are now colored in sepia—antiquated terms once used by doctors in frock coats and top hats. Janet inspired the Surrealist French poets to try automatic writing to unleash the creativity of the unconscious. The nineteenth-century medium Hélène Smith practiced automatic writing in a trance state and claimed that the texts that resulted were communications from Martians. The practice has been tainted by its association with hypnosis, poetry, and the occult, and no doubt by time itself. We suffer from the hubris of the present: with our misguided notion of perpetual progress, we believe that we are always moving forward and getting better and smarter.

During automatic writing, the person does not feel in control of what he writes. I didn't write the text; it was written for me. The phenomenon might be called literate alien hand syndrome. The feeling that words are being dictated to the writer rather than actually composed, however, is not lost in the past. Many poets, Blake and Yeats among them, but also more contemporary figures, such as James Merrill and Theodore Roethke, felt they were given verses from spirits or from the dead or simply as lightning bolts of sudden inspiration. Among writers, I would argue, this is not extraordinary but fairly common. When I am writing well, I often lose all sense of composition; the sentences come as if I hadn't willed them, as if they were manufactured by another being. This is not my day-to-day mode of writing, which includes grinding, painful periods of starts and stops. But the sense that I have been taken over happens several times during the course of a book, usually in the latter stages. I don't write; I am written. Were I prone to mystical explanations, I might imagine that an angel (or devil) had played with my typing fingers. My point is not to summon cherubim or demons but to naturalize something that has become taboo in the scientific community. What is at work in automatic writing? Unconscious self-suggestion? An incubated text that suddenly appears in words? Subliminal memories reconfigured and made conscious? Surely there is a relation between the neurological cases of Neil and Zazetsky and the possessed poets. But for the *Brain* authors, automatic writing becomes "a dissociative phenomenon that was *once* the subject of intensive study in both experimental and clinical psychology" (my italics). Not anymore. Knowledge does not always accumulate; it also gets lost. Valuable insights are thrown out with patently false ones. Neil's case becomes an isolate.

Nevertheless, in a textbook, *Psychiatric Issues in Epilepsy*, I find Janet mentioned in a section called "Toward a Conceptualization of Nonepileptic Seizures." And, under possible interventions and treatments, hypnosis is included along with other therapies. The authors restate a somewhat softer version of Charcot's controversial idea: "Hypnotizability can be a measure of dissociability and the degree of hypnotizability may be characteristic of differing psychopathological states." To say this plainly: the easier you are to hypnotize, the more likely you are to dissociate. Moreover, the book's authors relate that PET scans have "suggested a neurophysiological overlap between conversion symptoms and hypnosis with the finding of increased regional cerebral blood flow in both conditions, for example in the orbitofrontal and anterior cingulate regions."[69] So, as both Charcot and Janet posited, hysteria may be a kind of unconscious self-suggestion or self-hypnosis. According to this textbook and the research it cites, Charcot's neurological hypothesis about hysteria was not so far off as has been supposed.

It seems to me that going backward sometimes means going forward. The search for the shaking woman takes me round and round because in the end it is also a search for perspectives that may illuminate who and what she is. My only certainty is that I cannot be satisfied with looking at her through a single window. I have to see her from every angle.

HYSTERICS SUFFER MAINLY FROM REMINISCENCES. What is the role of memory in conversion disorder? The *DSM* does not mention Charcot, Janet, or Freud by name, but the authors do refer vaguely to the illness's past: "Traditionally, the term *conversion* derived from the hypothesis that the individual's somatic symptom represents a symbolic resolution of an unconscious psychological conflict, reducing anxiety and serving to keep the conflict out of awareness."[70] Note that they don't comment on its value as an idea or mention that memory may be involved. That remains outside the manual's task. They do say that if symptoms appear in "a close temporal relation" to "a conflict or stressor," this may help make a diagnosis. They also note, "Conversion disorder appears to be more frequent in women than in men, with reported ratios varying from 2:1 to 10:1."[71] Perhaps they should have added *in noncombat populations.*

Inexplicable paralyses, seizures, blindness, mutism, aphasias, and deafness have long been documented among soldiers, who, until recently, were all men. The largest number of reported cases was during and after the First World War, when shell-shock victims were legion. Life in the trenches was horror. The soldiers were immobilized. As they huddled in their long, narrow holes, they knew that at any moment they could be blasted to bits. A theme that links one case of conversion after another is that its victims suffer from a feeling of vulnerability and impotence. Events overwhelm them. They control nothing. When soldiers were allowed to move from the trenches and felt less trapped, the incidence of shell shock diminished considerably.[72] C. S. Myers described a classic example of war hysteria: An English soldier was in a trench with three other men when a shell hit, killing two of his comrades instantly and hurling him and the other survivor to the far end of the trench. Although he wasn't visibly injured, he couldn't stand up or speak coherently. At the field hospital, he fell into a stupor for seventeen days, woke up, and shouted, "They're at it again. Did you see that one, Jim?" He then relapsed, and when he came to again, he was both deaf and mute. He returned to England and lived in that state "until one day he had a hysteric, convulsive seizure, after which he shouted orders given in the trenches and thereupon regained his hearing and speech."[73]

The neuropsychiatrist Ed Weinstein wrote about conversion disorder among U.S. troops from the Civil War through Vietnam. During the Civil War, Weinstein contends, "a considerable number of the 28.3% discharges for epilepsy, and of the 20.8% for paralysis involved conversion disorders."[74] The reason for this claim is simple: many of those discharged returned home and made full recoveries. Hysteria and war go together. The problem is one of vocabulary and the magic of naming. If you give it another name, it appears to be another *thing*. Military physicians were loath to label their men with an illness that had always been associated with women. How could fighting men be hysterics? Moreover, as we have seen, medical history changes, and many, if not most doctors have little grasp of what came before their own contemporary frames for diagnosis.

They are incapable of drawing parallels with the past. A more recent case in an Israeli study makes this difficulty more apparent. The researchers analyzed thirty-four instances of patients admitted to the unit and diagnosed with "conversion paralysis motor disorder." In 1973, an army officer "with considerable battlefield experience" suffered an injury when his armored vehicle hit a land mine. He was taken to neurosurgery, fully conscious, but unable to move his legs. A CT scan showed no explanation for the paralysis, and the staff noticed that while he was asleep, his lower limbs seemed to have greater mobility. The patient improved, was transferred to Psychiatry, and after three weeks of therapy, left the hospital symptom free.

The man was diagnosed with "a conversion reaction as a result of post traumatic stress disorder, PTSD."[75] The diagnosis is puzzling. Here the man's hysterical symptoms are subsumed by PTSD, even though he manifested *only* conversion. Why? It might be that once he was in the psychiatric unit, his doctors unearthed other symptoms (although there is no mention of them, only of his steady recovery) or simply that his war record suggested that diagnosis to the doctors. The *DSM* does not mention conversion *as part of* PTSD, despite the abundant literature that connects it to trauma. The authors state, "If the symptom meets criteria for another mental disorder (e.g., Brief Psychotic Disorder, Conversion Disorder, Major Depressive Disorder), these diagnoses should be given instead of, or in addition to, Post-traumatic Stress Disorder."[76] Would a woman like Justine Etchevery, who had suffered a sexual attack, severe burns, and two near-fatal illnesses, have been diagnosed today with conversion as a result of PTSD? Was the Israeli offi- cer's diagnosis essentially associative, an added-on relative: battle-scarred veteran equals PTSD? Does PTSD's powerful connection to warfare give it a dignity that conversion couldn't possibly have because it has always been and still is linked to women?

During the Vietnam War, PTSD became the abbrevia- tion of choice to encapsulate the many traumatic symptoms that remained with soldiers after the war. Every war seems to call for its own name. Soldier's heart, shell shock, battle fatigue, war neurosis, and *Kriegsnervose* are all variants on the theme of psychic trauma due to the horror of battle. Obviously, memory plays an important role in the lives of soldiers who suffer from conversions. Unbearable memo- ries. Unwanted memories. Unwanted realities. Repression. Unconscious memories and ideas.

HOW FAR HAS SCIENCE come in understanding what is going on with people who have *psychogenic* symptoms— symptoms of many kinds that don't fit into ordinary neuro- logical diagnoses? In their 2006 paper "Conversion Disorder and fMRI" published in *Neurology,* Trevor H. Hurwitz and James W. Pritchard review a recent brain-scan study of hys- terics. At the end of their discussion, the authors reach 130 years into the past, to the English physician J. Russell Reynolds, "who described paralysis and other disorders of motion and sensation based on an 'idea which should take possession of the mind and lead to its own fulfillment.'"

They go on to "reformulate" that statement in contemporary terms: "conversion reactions are fixed beliefs of somatic dysfunction arising from psychological distress that control cortical and subcortical pathways to produce patterns of loss or gain of function that are not organic in the conventional sense."[77] Jean-Martin Charcot was present when Reynolds gave the paper cited by Hurwitz and Pritchard, at an 1869 conference of the British Medical Association in England, and the English physician's words had a powerful influence on the French neurologist, which he himself credited often and went on to develop.[78] "Fixed beliefs" sounds very much like Janet's "fixed idea, *idée fixe.*" Charcot, Janet, and Freud also knew that hysteria wasn't organic in the conventional sense. As far as I can tell from the many studies and papers I have tracked down, scientific ideas about hysteria have not advanced a single inch since the work done by these doctors in the late nineteenth and early twentieth centuries. Two authors of another paper on conversion and neuroimaging put it this way: "However, the question of how special psychological processes transmute into neurobiology has yet to be answered."[79] Wasn't this Freud's question, precisely, the one he hoped to answer in his *Project* in 1895?

There is general agreement that "psychological stressors" play a role in the symptoms of psychogenic illnesses, and now brain scans show clear evidence of neural changes in likely brain areas, but any broader explanation is lacking. What does it mean when Hurwitz and Prichard say "not organic in the conventional sense"? This seems true, but fuzzy. *Organic* has been used to designate illnesses that have a known cause, where seizure activity can be seen and measured, for example, or blindness can be attributed to a brain lesion, but *not* for those that can't. The advent of visible signs of conversion in people's brains seems to have left many researchers in a theoretical vacuum. What they're left with is something organic in the *unconventional* sense.

The mind/body problem is still so vexing, so entrenched as a duality that it becomes almost impossible to think without it. This split, after all, created the distinction between psychiatry and neurology: sick minds versus sick brains. Hysteria, once within the providence of neurology, was pushed into psychiatry. Nevertheless, by all accounts, most conversion patients first present themselves to neurologists because they appear to have neurological problems. The issue here is again one of perception and its frames, disciplinary windows that narrow the view. Without categories, we can't make sense of anything. Science has to control and restrict its windows or it will discover nothing. At the same time, it needs guiding thoughts and interpretation or its findings will be meaningless. But when researchers are trapped in preordained frames that allow little air in or out, imaginative science is smothered. Conversion studies are often small because it isn't easy to round up people with the same symptoms, and if described at all, the cases are usually tossed off in a couple of lines, as seen with another patient of the seven who participated in the *Brain* study:

Patient V.A.

Fifty-one-year-old, right-handed woman, divorced,

whose son died from heart disease a year prior to the study. Heaviness, weakness, and loss of dexterity of right limbs after her new companion suffered myocardial infarction while wrongly suspected of abusing a teenager. No sensory complaints.[80]

Poor V.A. Imagine the grief of losing a child to heart problems and then falling in love with a man who has a *heart* attack after being *falsely* accused of what appears to be the violence against or sexual molestation of some young person. She suffered too many blows involving hearts: her heart and the hearts of beloved others. The heart is the metaphorical location of love, after all. She fell ill with a broken heart. The word "while" suggests some ongoing investigation the couple had to endure, a lowering black cloud they woke up to every morning and went to bed with every night. Most cases of hysteria don't present themselves as madness. Like many psychiatric patients, these people have been subjected to repeated "stressors," but they don't have psychotic breaks and go howling into the streets. They are not immobilized by depression. Their symptoms are a metaphorical expression for what they can't say: *It's too much. I can't bear up. If I really pour out my grief and sadness, I'll fall apart.* I have often thought about the sentences written by D. W. Winnicott, an English psychoanalyst and pediatrician: "Flight to sanity is not health. Health is tolerant of ill health; in fact, health gains much from being in touch with ill health with all its aspects."[81] I understand him to mean that health can tolerate some disintegration. At one time or another all of us go to pieces, and it isn't necessarily a bad thing. That state of disunity may allow a flexible and open creativity that is part of being healthy.

One finding in this study that included V.A. and V.U., the Algerian woman who fled her country after members of her family were murdered, interested me very much. The authors write, "Remarkably, the same premotor circuits [the neural networks shown to be affected in the seven conversion patients] are also involved in unilateral motor neglect after organic neurological damage, where voluntary limb use may fail despite a lack of true paralysis and intact primary sensorimotor pathways."[82] After injury to the right parietal lobe, some patients suffer from *neglect*. They stop noticing the left side of space, including the left side of their own bodies. For example, a person with this problem will comb only the hair on the right side of her head, eat only from the right side of her plate, and if asked to draw a flower will draw only half of it—the right half. The left side has ceased to exist. *Hemiakinesia* is the motor form of neglect. A patient will fail to use her left arm and leg even though they should be, from a neurological point of view, capable of working. One such patient would sometimes hop on her right leg when she walked, but other times, she was able to use both.[83] Neglect is usually understood as a problem of *attention,* which is regarded as crucial to perception. One side of the world vanishes. Neglect patients sometimes deny that they have a paralyzed left arm, for example, and when it is shown to them will say that it belongs to another person, the physician or somebody else in the room, rather than claim it as their own. It has become an alien limb. The authors are drawing a connection between hysterical symptoms and hemiakinesia because they appear to involve the same premotor areas of the brain. The idea that organic and nonorganic illnesses (in the conventional sense) could mirror each other neurobiologically strikes them as remarkable.

Right-hemispheric damage often results in the syndromes I have mentioned before: denial of illness, anosognosia or what neurologists call *anosodiaphoria,* the admission of illness but without concern: Janet's *la belle indifférence,* which we saw in Todd Feinberg's patient Lizzy, who didn't seem to give a jot about her blindness, even when she admitted to it, and neglect. It is weird but true that if you pour cold water into the left ear of a neglect patient, the anosognosia will disappear. A patient of V. S. Ramachandran's did not acknowledge that she was paralyzed on the left side and that her left arm was effectively useless. Mrs. M. insisted that she was fine, could walk, could use both her hands, and when forced to look at the dead left hand claimed that it belonged to her son.[84] After her doctor poured ice water into her ear, she freely admitted her paralysis and acknowledged that her body had been that way ever since her stroke. Ramachandran confessed that witnessing the phenomenon made him take Freud's idea of repression seriously for the first time. It was obvious that at an unconscious level Mrs. M. *knew* she was paralyzed, but on a conscious level she did not *want* to know.

Karen Kaplan-Solms and Mark Solms cite Ramachandran's experiment in their book *Clinical Studies in Neuro-*

psychoanalysis. In one chapter, they describe five patients with right hemisphere damage. Each patient was treated neurologically but was also given psychotherapy. Although their lesions were not unalike (they all had right perisylvian damage), each person had a unique response to his or her injuries. Nevertheless, they all showed various forms of re-pressing or denying the bad news that they were no longer the same as they had been before. Their responses contrast sharply to Zazetsky's, who had left hemisphere damage and was, from the beginning, acutely and painfully aware of what he had lost. He repressed nothing. Neil, too, under-stood that he was forgetful and knew well that after his tu-mor and the radiation to shrink it, he had changed. It is easy to conclude that right-sided injuries create a fundamental inability in these people to know what has gone wrong with them. But the authors disagree: "These patients are indeed continuously encoding information about their defective bodies, and at some deeper level they do indeed have knowl-edge about their handicaps and the emotional implica-tions thereof. All that they lack is the capacity—or as we are suggesting—the inclination to attend to this knowledge, to permit it into conscious awareness." Or, to repeat Janet's words: *In reality what has disappeared . . . is the faculty that enables the subject to say clearly, "It is I who feel, it is I who hear."* It is I who am ill. It is I who remembers.

One of these patients, Mr. D., had suffered a cerebral hemorrhage but had made an impressive recovery. He had mild deficits on his left side, most of which were concen-trated in an unwieldy left hand that was also subject to involuntary twitching. The authors point out that although Mr. D. had for a time denied his illness and neglected his left side after the bleeding in his brain, these symptoms had subsided. In its place, he developed a virulent hatred for his own left hand: "I'll smash this hand into a million pieces and post the pieces to the surgeon, in envelopes, one by one." The authors comment, "At one point, Mr. D. actually stated that the hand felt as if it did not belong to him. The hand thus represented some part of his own self that he had both *lost* and *disowned*. An analysis of his attitudes in this regard suggested that, in fact, he was trying to turn the *passive* experience of losing it into an *active* experience of disowning it."[85] Rather than neglect the bad hand, not admit that it was there or that it belonged to him, he wanted to expel it from his "I," to refuse to accept that it was part of him.

Some of the other patients Kaplan-Solms and Solms studied displayed both denial of illness and *la belle indifférence,* but during sessions their analyst noticed that her patients' blasé attitudes faltered. Mrs. B., who declared that she had come to terms with the handicaps that remained after her stroke, was subject to severe crying jags, which she insisted she didn't understand, but when the catalysts were examined—an article about a thalidomide child born without limbs, for example—it was plain that she had been reminded of what she had lost. Her indifference masked what she understood in another part of herself and served as a shield against unbearable feelings. Another woman, who had neglect, anosognosia, and multiple visual and spatial difficulties, Mrs. A., explained her severe depression by saying that she kept "losing things," things like her glasses and cigarettes. But with her analyst she associated these minor losses to much greater ones: the loss of her uterus in a hysterectomy when she was still a young woman and the loss of her father when she was only a girl. She is quoted as saying, "I was never able to mourn the loss of my father."[86] One loss becomes linked to another and then another. There are too many. It is much easier to fret over missing glasses and cigarettes. Solms and Kaplan-Solms use their cases to argue against specific neurological theories that explain neglect and anosognosia by stating that the injuries sustained by patients like theirs create decreased emotion and a stunted awareness of their bodies and therefore a genuine inability *at any level* to know how bad things are. Their cases suggest that this isn't true, that something far more complex is going on.

Neglect and denial of illness seem to redraw the boundaries of the body and liberate the conscious "I" from having to worry about the *bad parts*. Mr. D. tried to remap himself without his malfunctioning hand, which he threatened to cut off and replace with a mechanical prosthesis. Conversion patients, on the other hand, seem unconsciously to create a bad body part or disability to take the blow instead of the "I," so it can go on its merry way unaffected. What about people with motor neglect, who should be able to use their limbs but don't? What about conversion patients who might be said to have the same functional possibility, since no physiological damage confirms their problem, but still can't use some part of their bodies? Why would the *Brain* study find subcortical similarities between people with hemiakinesia and conversion patients with weak or paralyzed limbs? The SPECT scans showed abnormalities in sensory and motor pathways that directly corresponded to the hysterical symptoms. These premotor loops or circuits (that involve the basal ganglia and the thalamus) are known to be crucial for *intentional* movements. Their activation may also be part of a *subjective* sense of *voluntary* movement. *I* am moving. When stimulated directly, these same brain areas can trigger movements that the subject feels he or she has *willed*. (Of course, it is not known how that subjectivity actually develops in neural terms.) And a person who sustains a lesion, say, from a stroke may end up with hemiakinesia and "forget" that he can use both legs to walk. These are areas then that have been linked to motor volition, to the ownership of movements. I, not you, am moving my hand. That they are implicated in both conversion and hemiakinesia makes sense because in both there is a derangement of a feeling of subjective ownership of parts of the body.

Exactly how this sense of ownership of our bodies functions remains mysterious, as does what consciousness actually is and certainly how it works and what it's *for*. In the 1980s, the neuroscientist Benjamin Libet did many experiments that demonstrated, against most people's deepest intuitions, that up to half a second before we make a conscious decision to act, move a wrist or finger, for example, the brain precedes the movement with an electrical change called a "readiness potential," an RP, which can be measured. In short, his experiments suggested that *the brain initiates voluntary acts unconsciously.*[87] The controversy over these findings has understandably been nothing short of tremendous. Neuroscientists, philosophers, and other concerned citizens have all weighed in. Are we nothing but automata? Do we have free will? The debate over this question is very old, and human beings understandably cling to the idea that we choose what we do. In 1748, Julian de La Mettrie argued in *L'Homme Machine* that states of the soul are dependent on states of the body and that unconscious, involuntary processes can be separated from conscious, voluntary processes only because the latter are more complex.[88] Are we in charge of our destinies or do we simply believe that we decide our own actions? And what mechanism decides that we are deciding? Libet's discovery alarmed him. His position, arrived at through his research, is that while we may not will our movements, we can veto or inhibit them. In other words, conscious free will may function as a big No. No, I'm not going to hit you, even though I feel the urge coming. A great many moral decisions fall into this category.

On the other hand, perhaps free will is not something that has to be fully conscious. Our body schema, after all, is mostly unconscious. When I open the refrigerator to get a drink, the gesture is so automatic I barely think about it, and am I not doing it because I'm thirsty? Am I conscious of the thirst in the sense that I have to announce to myself, "I am *now conscious* of my thirst" before I go for the drink? No, but I have to be aware of thirst somehow, even though it's not acknowledged in a full-blown self-reflexive sentence that bears the pronoun "I." And I certainly don't have to see myself from the outside as the hero of my life to get the bottle of water. The neuroscientist Jaak Panksepp has identified various emotional systems in the brains of all mammals, including what he calls "the SEEKING system." "This system," he writes, "makes animals intensely interested in exploring their world and leads them to become excited when they are about to get what they desire."[89] We all look for what we need and want, including taking out the water from the refrigerator. Because some part of my unconscious self prepares in advance for my water-getting gesture, does it mean that I don't want it, that I am a machine of automatic motions?

Perhaps it would be useful to describe degrees of consciousness. After all, even when I'm writing, much is generated unconsciously. I feel beneath my words a preconscious world from which I draw them, thoughts not yet articulated but potentially there, and when I find them, I believe in their rightness or wrongness. Yes, that's what I wanted to say. Against what do I measure this? It is not *outside* me. I don't have some externalized notion of the perfect sentence that best expresses what I want to say. The knowledge lives inside me, and yet, isn't that verbal interior made from the exterior, from all the books I've read, the conversations I've had and their mnemic traces? I like the expressions "in the back of my mind" and "on the tip of my tongue," which indicate that half-remembered underground. What actually happens when I write the symbols that together make up the words *I remember*?

Subjectivity is not the story of a stable, absolute "I" that marches through life making one conscious decision after another. It is not a disembodied brain machine either, genetically preprogrammed to act in specified and predictable ways. The once popular model of the brain as a computer hard drive that is fed software has grown weaker over time. The computer became a cognitive model with the advent of the technology, and I find it rather odd that scientists and a good many philosophers should decide that a machine is an adequate model for the human mind. For one thing, machines aren't emotional, and without affective values, human beings can't make decisions. They lose rather than gain good judgment. In his book *Descartes' Error,* Antonio Damasio gives neurological evidence for what many people know intuitively, that emotion is crucial to reasoning well.[90] People with frontal lobe injuries have blunted emotions, and this affects their ability to act for their own welfare. Furthermore, our subjectivity is not closed but open to the outside world. This is indisputable, but strangely, it's often forgotten, and the scientific fetish for brain function sometimes treats these processes as if they took place in an isolated, bodiless organ—a bunch of neurons in a vat going about its business alone. "All action," William James wrote, "is thus re-action upon the outer world; and the middle stage of consideration or contemplation or thinking is only a place of transit, the bottom of a loop, both whose ends have their point of application in the outer world. . . . The current of life which runs in at our eyes or ears is meant to run out at our hands, feet or lips."[91] James's model of subjective experience is dynamic, and it includes the perceived world, with all that means—sights, sounds, smells, sensations, emotions, other people, thought, and language. These are *in us*. We are inhabited, occupied, plural, and always live in relation to that perceived external world as corporeal beings, not just brains.

Edmund Husserl, whose phenomenology was influenced by his reading of James, made a distinction between two senses of the body: *Körper* and *Leib*.[92] *Körper* is our physical body, a thing, the one that can be seen from a third-person point of view in medicine and science as an inert object or "it." *Körper* is what can be dissected. *Leib* is the lived body, the animated first-person psychobiological experiencing being. We can find *Körper* in *Gray's Anatomy*. We find *Leib* in ourselves, the embodied "I."

THE SUBJECTIVE WORLD is also an intersubjective world, the world of "I" and "you," and drawing a line between the two isn't easy because others are *of us*. It is now known that infants as young as a few hours old will actively imitate the expressions of an adult looking at them. This appears to be an inborn trait. It is not that newborn babies have a body image of their own faces moving to mimic the faces of others. They are not self-conscious. They are not yet the heroes of their own lives, but they have a powerful response to faces. After my daughter was born, I spent hours just looking at her, and she looked at me. I couldn't get enough of that child's face and her large, attentive eyes that locked into mine. My mother once said about me and my sisters, "When you were children, I feasted on your faces." This phrase is a good summary of the emotion communicated by the maternal gaze because it focuses on the pleasure of looking, on the *need* to do it. Very small babies, only weeks old, will also answer you. I have experimented with this many times. If you speak to an infant and wait (you have to give her time), she will make talking sounds in response. The beginnings of language are in imitation. We are mirrors of one another.

D. W. Winnicott writes, "In emotional development the precursor of the mirror is the mother's face."[93] He mentions the importance of Lacan's essay "Le Stade de Miroir," but points out that Lacan does not make the same connection between the maternal and the mirror: "What does the baby see when he or she looks at the mother's face? I am suggesting that ordinarily, what the baby sees is himself or herself. *In other words the mother is looking at the baby and what she looks like is related to what she sees there.*"[94] I am reflected in your eyes. In the same essay, Winnicott makes this formulation:

> When I look I am seen, so I exist
> I can now afford to look and see
> I now look creatively and what I apperceive I also perceive
> In fact, I take care not to see what is not there to be seen
>   (unless I am tired).[95]

Our eyes are directly connected to our brains, which helps explain why we are always looking into the eyes of other people to discover what they mean. As E. H. Hess wrote, the eye is "anatomically an extension of the brain; it is almost as if a portion of the brain were in plain sight."[96] Neurobiologists know that these visual exchanges between mother and child facilitate brain development in the infant. Allan Schore calls the back-and-forth between mother and child "psychobiological attunement" and, following others, refers to mother and baby with the single noun *dyad*—a loop, two in one. "The mother's emotionally expressive face is the most potent source of visuoaffective information," he notes, "and in face to face interactions it serves as a visual imprinting stimulus for the infant's developing nervous system."[97] Our lives begin as a wordless dialogue, and without it we won't grow.

It is impossible to separate nature and nurture. You cannot isolate a person from the world in which he lives, but more than that, notions of outside and inside, subject and object become entwined. *The current of life that runs in at our eyes and ears is meant to run out at our hands, feet, and lips.* We are made through others, and this early motion of recognitions between child and mother and then, somewhat later, child and father is essential to who we become, and to our mature sense of a body image, a formed bodily identity. Shaun Gallagher writes, "It is in the intermodal and intersubjective interaction between proprioception [our mostly unconscious motor body schema] and the vision of the other's face that one's [conscious] body image develops."[98] In my words, children must acquire an "I" through a "you." They are born with a genetic temperament—high-strung and sensitive, for example, or relatively calm and docile—that will influence how they react to visual and emotional stimuli, and they have all the necessary tools to become part of the interacting, speaking world, but the conscious, articulated "I" isn't a given. Its arrival is part of an extended corporeal developmental process that involves mirrorings and mutual recognitions.

Many people have by now heard of mirror neurons discovered in 1995 by Vittorio Gallese, Giacomo Rizzolatti, Leonardo Fogassi, and Luciano Fadiga in macaque monkeys.[99] These neurons, located in the animal's premotor cortex fire when the monkey does something, grasps a banana, for example, but they also fire when the monkey watches the same action but does nothing. Not surprisingly, scientists have identified a mirror system in human beings. Exactly what this all means isn't known, but the discovery of mirror neurons has created speculation that they are involved in everything from language to empathy. Rizzolatti believed he had found the underlying signaling system of human language. At the very least, mirror neurons appear to be part of the dialectical back-and-forth inherent in human relations, a biological root for the reflexivity of "I" and "you," an idea that can be traced at least back to Hegel and resonates strongly with his understanding that our self-consciousness is rooted in relations between the self and other: "Self-consciousness exists in itself and for itself, in that, and by the fact that it exists for another self-consciousness; that is so to say only by being acknowledged or 'recognized.'"[100]

The word "I" appears rather late in children's speech. As Merleau-Ponty points out, "The pronoun I has its full meaning only when the child uses it not as an individual sign to designate his own person—a sign that would be given once for all to himself and nobody else—but when he understands that each person he sees is an 'I' for himself and a 'you' for others."[101] Before the "I" comes, most children refer to themselves by their proper names. I remember my daughter saying, "Sophie carrot" for "I want a carrot." Luria's six-year-old twins had no word in their private language for "I." They referred to themselves in the third person. In some forms of aphasia, the "I" vanishes early, and with some schizophrenics "I" and "you" become confused or meaningless. In the memoir *Autobiography of a Schizophrenic Girl*, Renee writes about her illness, her delusions about a controlling System giving her orders, and the therapy that brought her back to "reality":

> What did me the most amazing good was her use of the third person in speaking of herself, "Mamma and Renee" [Renee called her therapist Mamma], not "I and you." When by chance she used the first person, abruptly I no longer knew her, and I was angry that she had, by this error, broken my contract with her. So that when she said, "You will see how together we shall fight against the System," (What were I and you?) for me, there was no reality. Only "Mamma" and "Renee" or, better still, "the little personage," contained reality, life, affectivity."[102]

Renee's psychosis disrupted far more than her language. Her whole ego organization had gone to pieces, but one sign of her disintegration was a regression to an earlier stage of language use, and a wobbling, empty "I." The third person, "Renee," and the descriptive phrase "the small personage" had a concrete reality, a fixity and objectivity she couldn't find in the mutability of "I" and "you," which depend exclusively on the speaker.

I tutored a disturbed girl who had a tendency to slip into the third person, not always, but at times. She had been abandoned by both her parents, had lived with several relatives, and had ended up in foster care. She had also been a victim of a sexual assault when she was eleven. "Linnie doesn't like school," she would say or "They hate Linnie." Once, she uttered the astounding sentence "If I had my father's love, then I would be the *real* Linnie." There were two Linnies, one loveless and unreal, the other loved and real. There are many ways to become unhinged, but repeated blows, losses, and deprivations often show themselves as identity problems: the I and the not-I or the I and the it, the real and the unreal. There are psychological aspects to neurological disorders as well, although how to distinguish them from the illness or localized brain damage is poorly understood. Mr. D. turned his morbid left hand into a vile "it." Alien hands no longer belong to the articulating "I." Who is acting in these cases? Neil's hand recorded memories his speaking "I" couldn't recall. Freud's word for the instinct-driven unconscious part of his triunal self was the It, *das Es,* which became "id" in English, a term he borrowed from Georg Groddeck, who wrote, "I hold the view that man is animated by the Unknown, that there is within

95

him an 'Es,' an 'It,' some wondrous force, which directs both what he himself does and what happens to him. The affirmation, 'I live' is only conditionally correct, it expresses only a small and superficial part of the fundamental principle, 'Man is lived by It.' "[103] Freud elaborated on Groddeck's concept to create a driven but ahistorical or timeless part of the self that we have no knowledge of. Benjamin Libet, who experimented with free will would probably agree. The internal "It" has force, but it doesn't *talk*.

THE DEEPEST INSTINCT we animals have is to survive. Our whole beings have been naturally selected to go on living and make more of us. All animals probably have a built-in sense of their own vulnerability and mortality. I am not one of those people who is afraid of attributing emotions to animals. Apparently, elephants mourn their dead. The neuroscientist D. O. Hebb discovered that monkeys shun *representations* of the severed heads of their simian relations, heads they know perfectly well aren't real. An awareness of threat and defensive behavior is crucial to survival, but we may be the only animals who are capable of contemplating our own deaths. And yet, few of us like to think about the end. We suppress it. When death comes close, as it did for me in the car accident, emotions shut down; in my case, the fear came howling back in involuntary blasts of horrific memory. I can't think of a better passage in literature about our repression of mortality than this one from Tolstoy's "The Death of Iván Ilých":

In the depth of his heart he knew he was dying, but not only was he not accustomed to the thought, he simply did not and could not grasp it.

The syllogism he had learnt from Kiesewetter's Logic: "Caius is a man, men are mortal, therefore Caius is mortal," had always seemed to him correct as applied to Caius, but certainly not as applied to himself. That Caius—man in the abstract—was mortal, was perfectly correct, but he was not Caius, not an abstract man, but a creature quite separate from all others. He had been little Ványa, with a mamma and a papa, with Mítya and Volódya, with the toys, the coachman and a nurse, afterwards with Kátenka and with all the joys, griefs, and delights of childhood, boyhood, and youth. What did Caius know of the smell of that striped leather ball Ványa had been so fond of? Had Caius kissed his mother's hand like that, and did the silk of her dress rustle so for Caius? Had he rioted like that at school when the pastry was bad? Had Caius been in love like that? Could Caius preside at a session as he did? Caius really was mortal, and it was right for him to die; but for me, little Ványa, Iván Ilých, with all my thoughts and emotions, it's altogether a different matter. It cannot be that I ought to die. That would be too terrible.[104]

The leap from Caius to little Ványa is from the abstract to the particular, from knowing something intellectually to not *really* knowing it, from general truth to personal truth, from a third-person reality to a first-person reality. The jump also takes us back in time, to the memories of early childhood, to the dear smell of a leather ball and to the sensual presence of a mother, to a world that revolved around little Ványa, His Majesty the baby, the beloved little boy. It is so ordinary, this denial of the inevitable, the thing that must come, the end of me, but how hard it is to truly comprehend. Tolstoy uses the pronoun *It* to describe the lurking presence in the life of Iván Ilých, one our hero desperately tries to avoid. He looks for "consolations—new screens—and new screens were found and for a while seemed to save him, but then they immediately fell to pieces or rather became transparent, as if *It* penetrated them and nothing could veil *It*." Like Mrs. A., who poured her grief into missing glasses and cigarettes, Iván Ilých worries over scratches on his polished table and a torn album and then falls into a quarrel with his wife and daughter over where to keep the damaged album, and finds that these trivial disputes are also saving screens: "But that was all right, for then he did not think about *It*. *It* was invisible."[105] *It* denotes an alien, the not-I, whether the strange animal forces of desire and aggression that seem to live in us or the terrible reality that those powers aren't eternal, that they end in a corpse, in thingness, the inanimate, the once-I, now an it.

THE FIRST TIME I SHOOK I was standing on home ground. It wasn't only that my father had taught for many years at the college. As a child, I had lived on that campus because my professor father had a second job as head resident of a men's dormitory. That old building has since been torn down, but I remember its murky hallways, its smells, the elevator with its red door, the soda pop machine glowing on the floor below us, and the button on it for Royal Crown Cola. I remember the fat, kind janitor, Bud, with his dusty gray pants, the forbidden upper floors where my sister Liv and I ventured a couple of times. I remember the view from the window in our apartment, where I stood one Easter and cried. On that day of hats and gloves and light spring dresses, convention dictated warm and sunny, but what I saw through the window was snow. I remember when I learned to ride a bicycle on that same ground one spring, and the feeling I had when my father let go of the bike and I pedaled off alone, weaving a little, but joyous the moment I understood I had been released and was still upright. I remember the power plant, where my father took me and Liv through the billowing white smoke and the blast of heat and the roar of machinery into a small room near the back of the building where a man made ice cream and gave us samples for free. I remember lying over the grates outside the library and studying the candy wrappers and cigarette butts and various kinds of debris that had fallen down there, and how absorbing it was just to look at those things. We moved outside town before I entered the third grade, but aside from a few fragments from my third and fourth years, my autobiographical memory from five through nine is largely fixed on that campus. Places have power.

Did standing there on that familiar ground unleash the reality of death for me—the presence of an unspeakable *It*? After all, I live in New York and didn't see my father on a daily basis. In New York it was ordinary that he should be missing from my life. Was I thrown into a subliminal realization that his absence was permanent, irrevocable, without being consciously aware of the turn taken inside me? Did the faces of people I knew from my childhood hurl me back to an earlier self? Did the shuddering have something to do with occupying my father's place? Quite literally, standing in a place I felt belonged to him? Was the sight of that green lawn outside Old Main, where my father once had his office, the image of which is scratched into my memory because I walked there again and again, not only as a child but as a girl, and then as a young woman when I was a student? But it wasn't the vision of the place that started the convulsion; it was the act of speaking. It began with the first word and ended with the last. Was it connected to a memory?

EXPLICIT MEMORIES THRIVE ON PLACES. Classical theories argued that to do their work memories require locations—*topoi*. Cicero credited Simonides of Ceos for creating an art of memory. When an earthquake hit a banquet hall and killed everyone in the room, Simonides, who had been called away from the festivites, returned and was able to identify the crushed bodies because he remembered where each guest had been sitting. From this gruesome event, the story goes, Simonides discovered the essential connection between locality and memory. Through his reading of Aristotle, the scholastic philosopher Albertus Magnus (d. 1280) proposed that mental places serve a practical purpose for the mind and make it easier to retrieve memories. They are not mirrors of reality but, rather, internal conceptions of it.[106] Cicero developed the idea of *locus* as a tool for verbal memory. A speaker could memorize a long speech by visualizing a house and strolling through it, attaching each part of his talk to a different spot, a table or a rug or a door in the various rooms. My father used this technique to memorize his speeches, and it seemed to work well. Walking through an imagined architecture becomes the space in which one can fix sequential, verbal thoughts. Freud's commentary about the more primitive character of the visual mental image as opposed to words is pertinent. My visual memory is often rather static, and I remember best intimate places—houses, woods, fields, and streets I have memorized because they were experienced again and again as the backdrop of my life. They are spaces I have lived in or with over time.

On the other hand, a place I visited only once often grows dim. I may have a vague sense, a schema, if you will, of walking down a street in Hong Kong, for example, but what stands out in my memory is a beggar kneeling in the street who grabs the hem of my dress and I recoil. Repugnance, pity, and guilt visit me in turn, but the image of the man's face, which I know frightened me with its desperation, is no longer vivid. I can reinvent it in my mind's eye, as the apt saying goes. He has rotting teeth, bloodshot eyes, dirty cheeks. What I actually retain is the knowledge that it happened and that I have thought about it a number of times since, but the words I use to tell myself the story have supplanted any detailed picture. Hong Kong was filled with beggars in 1975. I remember this in a general, factual way, but I can no longer summon visual imagery that isn't a vague jumble reconfigured into an impressionistic, imprecise version of my experience. Language abstracts visual memory and, in time, often replaces it by creating a fixed narrative that can be repeated again and again.

A more striking example of place as the theater of memory can be found in an error I discovered about my own recollections. One of my earliest memories is from when I was four. It took place at my aunt's house in Bergen, Norway, at a family meal. The chief visual components of the incident consist of the familiar table in the familiar living room with its window overlooking the fjord. I can see that room clearly in my mind because, thirteen years later, I lived with my aunt and uncle in that house. I also recall a few definite, sequential movements. I was sitting in a chair across from my twelve-year-old cousin, Vibeke, whom I loved and admired, when suddenly, for reasons I didn't understand, she began to cry. I remember pushing myself off the chair. My legs didn't reach the floor, so I had to slip to the ground. I walked over to my cousin and patted her back in an effort to comfort her. The grown-ups began to laugh, and I was seized by burning humiliation. The memory has never left me. I now understand that the adults' laughter wasn't malicious, but the assault on my dignity has lasted, and it shaped my motherhood with my own daughter. I remembered, to quote Joe Brainard, "that life was just as serious then as it is now," that children must be respected as well as loved. The mistake I made was not about my emotion but about *where* I had been when my pride was wounded.

This bump to my self-esteem could not possibly have taken place in the house I remembered because when I was four years old *that house had not yet been built*. I reassigned the memory to a place I could remember, rather than the one I had forgotten. As Albertus Magnus argued: the room served a useful purpose. I needed to root the event somewhere in order to retain it. It required a visual home or it would float away unanchored. Like the ancient and medieval memory experts, I attached my now mostly verbal scenario to a *locus*.

Another of A. R. Luria's patients, S., whom the neurologist studied for thirty years and wrote about in his book *The Mind of a Mnemonist: A Little Book About a Vast Memory*, had the ability to convert lengthy lists of numbers and words into mental pictures of places:

> When S. read through a long series of words, each word would elicit a graphic image. And since the series was fairly long, he had to find some way of distributing these images of his in a mental row or sequence. Most often (and this habit persisted throughout his life), he would "distribute" them along some roadway or street he visualized in his mind. Sometimes this was a street in his home town, which would also include the yard attached to the house he had lived in as a child and which he recalled vividly. On the other hand, he might also select a street in Moscow. Frequently, he would take a mental walk along that street— Gorky Street in Moscow—beginning at Mayakovsky Square, and slowly making his way down, "distributing" his images at houses, gates, and store windows. At times,

without realizing how it had happened, he would find himself back in his hometown (Torzhok), where he would wind up his trip in the house where he had lived as a child. The setting he chose for his "mental walks" approximates that of dreams, the difference being that the setting in his walks would immediately vanish once his attention was distracted but would reappear just as suddenly when he was obliged to recall a series he had "recorded" in this way.[107]

Luria doesn't mention the classical systems, nor did S. study Cicero. His memory came to him naturally, as it were, a product of his synesthesia, which is a crossing of senses—tasting colors, for example, or seeing sounds. The great physicist Richard Feynman saw equations in color: "When I see equations, I see the letters in colors—I don't know why . . . light tan j's, slightly violet-bluish u's and dark brown x's flying around."[108]

The first stanza of Rimbaud's poem "Vowels" gives a perfect evocation of this form of synesthesia:

Black A, white E, red I, green U, blue O—vowels
Some day I will open your silent pregnancies:
A, black belt, hairy with bursting flies,
Bumbling and buzzing over stinking cruelties.[109]

S.'s prodigious memory was the result of his vivid internal visual perceptions. The man saw everything. "Even numbers remind me of images," he explained. "Take the number 1. This is a proud well-built man; 2 is a high-spirited woman, 3 a gloomy person (why, I don't know), 6 a man with a swollen foot."[110] The enormous scope of S.'s memory, however, was in many ways a hindrance to understanding the world around him. He had difficulty following stories and poems, because every word he read would produce an elaborate visual image. By the time he made his way to the end of a sentence he was thoroughly confused by the myriad, detailed, and competing pictures that cluttered his mind. A list of unrelated numbers or words was therefore far more conducive to his gifts, because each entity could exist as an isolate. By turning every sign into a concrete visual image, he became unable to grasp their meanings abstractly and so lacked the ability to distinguish between what was important and unimportant. The hierarchies of semantics vanished in a visual democracy. S. resembles no one so much as the hero of Jorge Luis Borges's story "Funes the Memorious."

> He was, let us not forget, almost incapable of ideas of a general, Platonic sort. Not only was it difficult for him to comprehend that the generic symbol dog embraces so many unlike individuals of diverse size and form, it bothered him that the dog at three fourteen (seen from the side) should have the same name as the dog at three fifteen (seen from the front). His own face in the mirror, his own hands, surprised him every time he saw them.

Near the end of the story, the narrator comments on the hero, "I suspect, however, that he was not very capable of thought. To think is to forget differences, generalize, make abstractions."[111] Unlike Funes, whose visual memory was perfect, S. found it hard to remember people's faces (proposagnosia) or register the emotions on those faces, something now associated with both autism and lesions that affect a particular part of the brain vital to face recognition, the fusiform gyrus. His extraordinary skills as well as his deficits would today earn S. not only the descriptive designation "synesthete," but also a diagnosis: Asperger's syndrome.

Perhaps it is not surprising that S. had a double, a third-person "he," who accompanied the mnemonist all his life. He projected his own persona into the landscape. As a child, S. would sometimes lie in bed and watch his double get dressed and go off to school in his place. When S. was eight, his family moved to a new apartment. Here is his description of that event. Note his use of the present tense. He recalls the event as he sees it again:

> I don't want to go. My brother takes me by the hand and leads me to the cab waiting outside. I see the driver there munching a carrot. But I don't want to go. . . . I stay behind in the house—that is, I see how "he" stands at the window of my old room. He's not going anywhere.[112]

Luria identifies this as a "split between an 'I' who issues orders and the 'he' who carries them out (whom the 'I' in S. visualized)." But the "he" is also the one who disobeys, who gets to stay in the dear old room after the "I" is dragged away. "He" fulfills the wishes of the "I." "He" is akin to a dream figure, which lacks the inhibition of the wakeful S. Even as an adult, S. explained, his double couldn't always be counted on to behave well:

> That is, I'd never say anything like that [a less than polite remark about the quality of his host's cigarettes], but "he" might. It's not tactful, but I can't explain that slip to him. For "I" understand things, but "he" doesn't. If I'm distracted, "he" says things he oughtn't to."[113]

In this case, "he" plays the imp of the perverse, the double role familiar from the characters of literature and clinical neurology, but we may all have latent or potential doubles, mirror images acting out what the "I" wants to suppress. Small children with imaginary friends who take the blame for mishaps or naughtiness or who must be consulted before the child obeys a parent are hardly unusual. And like S., every child thinks more concretely than a normal adult. I remember the confusion I felt when, on New Year's Eve, my parents would put my sisters and me to bed with the words "See you next year!" How a whole year could pass before morning was beyond my comprehension. Both Renee and my pupil Linnie were far more *concrete* in their thinking than most people their age and, like S., they lapsed into a third-person reality—the self as a "he" or a "she": "If I had my father's love, then I would be the *real* Linnie." My young writing patient B. also eschewed the "I" for a third-person account in her story about the exchanged notebooks and violent fathers. Isn't the "I"as "she" in any narrative a form of autoscopy? Like Luria's twins, Renee, Linnie, and maybe B., too, appear to be stuck in an earlier, less verbally developed, but more visual world. Isn't it reasonable to speculate that they never gained what some neurological patients have lost?

Luria understood that S.'s rich inner life compromised the generally recognized threshold between fantasy and reality. His mental life was so full that he would often get lost inside it. But S. not only remembered, he *imagined*. His erect number 1 and gloomy number 3 (the latter is downcast, I am sure, because the fellow's head is bent over) remind me of my own early personifications of just about everything that came into my visual field: breakfast cereal, sticks, stones, shoes. But then I have long believed that memory and imagination are two aspects of the same process. Neuroscientists now know that when we retrieve a memory, we find not the original memory but, rather, the one we summoned to consciousness the last time we remembered it. In this process, memories mutate. They are not only kept, *consolidated* in memory, they are re-kept, *reconsolidated*. Witness my unconscious transfer of a recollection from one house to another. It wasn't my visuospatial sense that detected my mistake—my humiliation scenario is still staged in that *second* living room. I have no other convenient place to put it. My recourse to the "truth" of the matter was rational. I recognized the logical impossibility that the scene I had been playing out in my mind had taken place where I *saw* it.

A friend of mine told me a story about his wife. A Jewish girl who went to a Catholic high school, she was faced with a conundrum on the day of her graduation. After every young woman received her diploma, it was customary for her to kiss the ring of the priest who had handed her the official paper. J. decided to dispense with the ritual kiss on principle and later told the story of her small but significant act of nonconformity to her family and friends, with some pride. Years after the event, she happened to see a film of the graduation ceremony and was stunned to watch her younger self walk onto the stage, take her diploma, and bend over to kiss the priest's ring. J.'s error was neither knowing nor deceitful. Rather, it was an unconscious reimagining of the moment, which served an important restorative purpose for her self-image. At some point in her history the memory had been reconsolidated. Surely, her wish that the story be exactly the opposite of what had actually happened was part of the transformation—a psychobiological process, through which the actual was replaced by the imaginary: a screen or, rather, a double, a "she" acting out J.'s desire. The phenomenon scientists call *observer* memory, when a person recalls the past not as an embodied first-person self but as a third-person other, may well be a similar form of this division, the creation of an imaginary mirror double who performs on the stage of memory. I have often wondered how many of my own reminiscences are distortions or the products of an imagination so vivid they have come to seem true.

A hundred years before neuroscientists understood reconsolidation, Freud wrote that the present colors the past, that memories are not always what they seem and cannot be relied upon as factual. Some memories may be screens for others. And most crucially, people revise their memories at a later date. He called this *Nachträglichkeit*; the word is very hard to translate into English. James Strachey, Freud's translator, called it "deferred action," but it actually means something like "afterlyness."[114] An early memory takes on new meanings and changes as a person matures. The hippocampus is a part of the brain vital for episodic memory and has also been tied to aspects of spatial memory.[115] It develops postnatally, which is a physiological explanation for infantile amnesia, the fact that our first years are lost in a fog. We have implicit memories from our earliest years, but not explicit ones, and it seems more than likely that for any experience to be recovered as a conscious memory, it once had to have been conscious. So people who claim to remember their births or powerful experiences that occurred in the first two years of their lives are more than likely in the grip of fantasies. My curiosity about the role language plays in building conscious memories has led me to quiz people about what they remember from their early childhoods. The results of my thoroughly unscientific survey are that without exception those who said they started talking at a very young age also have the earliest explicit recollections. This is true in my own family. My sister Asti, who was speaking in fluent sentences before the age of two, remembers far more from her third year of life than her three sisters.

There is now general agreement that memory is both shifting and creative. A study of people with bilateral hippocampal lesions found that the damage impaired not only their memories but their imaginations. The researchers asked the people in the study to imagine fictional places and events. When the subjects were prompted to conjure up a new experience—lying on a beach or walking through a museum exhibit—the brain-damaged patients' descriptions were wan and impoverished, compared to the vivid, particular scenes produced by the "normal controls."[116] But even among so-called normal people, there is a wide range of imaginative differences.

When I read a novel, I see it, and later, I remember the images I invented for the book. Some of those images are borrowed from intimate places in my own life. Others, I suspect, are taken from movies or pictures in books or paintings I've seen. I need to *put* the characters somewhere. Many people I've spoken to confirm that they also *see* books. Once, however, I met a man on a panel with me, a poet and translator, who swore he did not invent images when he read. We were discussing Proust. "Well," I asked him, "if you don't see Marcel's room and his mother and all of the people in the story, what happens?" He answered, "I see the words." I was flabbergasted. It struck me as a sad way to read, but who knows? Perhaps his mind does not convert the symbols into pictures, and why would he feel the lack of something he has never known? When I write fiction, I see my characters moving around, speaking, and acting, and I always place them in actual rooms, houses, buildings, and streets I know and remember well. I am usually one of those characters, not I as I but I as someone else, an other self, male or female, projected into the mental world I inhabit as I write. Mostly, I don't bother to describe the familiar interiors and exteriors in any detail, but I need them in order to do the work. My fictional events have to be grounded in the same way as the experiences I remember. I need *loci*. I don't assume that all novelists work this way. Nevertheless, for many people, reading is a form of ordinary synesthesia. We turn abstract signs into visual scenes.

A young, gifted Mexican novelist, M., told me that while writing his first novel, he understood that he was making a house, room by room, and that when he finished, the house had been built. For him, the act of writing had precise visual coordinates. "I had the idea," he wrote to me in an e-mail, "that this novel is like a white house, a funny one, that contains a second house, a dark and sinister one. In the center of the second house there is a garden, and in the garden there are brave dogs and a gardener who waits for the reader to arrive so he can tell him a story." M. likes to get other novelists to draw a diagram or map of their novels, not unlike the little maps of narrative Laurence Sterne included in *Tristram Shandy*. When he asked me to do it for one of mine, I hesitated, but then the visual form arrived in my mind and I drew it quickly.

The faculty of memory cannot be separated from the imagination. They go hand in hand. To one degree or another, we all invent our personal pasts. And for most of us those pasts are built from emotionally colored memories. Affects give meaning to experience or *value*, as some philosophers put it. What we don't care about we forget. Indeed, our amnesia for many things is a blessing. S. had a terrible time trying to expell visions in that overstuffed mind of his. He simply stored too much. My memory of the trip across the floor to console my cousin made its way into my autobiography through emotion, in this case an indignity visited upon the all-important "little personage," *me*. Aristotle divided every memory into a likeness or visual image in the mind, *simulacrum,* and its emotional charge, *intentio.* The ancient philosopher understood that there was no memory without an accompanying affect. But when I search for a memory associated with speaking in public, I cannot find it. Am I frightened of something entirely hidden from me?

THE NEUROSCIENTIST Joseph LeDoux has done much of his research on fear and the circuits in the brain that are activated when a rat is repeatedly given an electric shock after hearing a tone. The animal quickly associates the tone with the shock, and once the connection is learned it will exhibit a fear response, freezing, when it hears the tone, even when the sound isn't followed by a shock. The rat remembers that tone means shock. If enough time goes by, however, without the combination of tone and shock, the animal's behavior may change, but the association between the neutral and the aversive stimuli will endure—possibly, LeDoux believes, for a lifetime. In this respect, human beings aren't different from rats. We, too, can learn fear. Since my accident, I have had a lingering alarm about traveling by car, one I don't have in planes or on boats. It is not rational. Being in one car crash does not predispose you to another, but the association of car with crash has been made, and it exhibits itself as a bodily tension, an anxiety that runs through me whenever I enter an automobile. At the same time, my fear has steadily diminished because I have managed to inhibit it by reasoning about my irrational fear, and I haven't been in another collision.

LeDoux's work recalls Pavlov's famous conditioning studies with dogs. The difference is that through similar training and with new tools, he has identified parts of the essential fear routes in the brain, involving, in particular, a small almond-shaped part of the limbic system called the amygdala, which is also involved in the consolidation and reconsolidation of emotional memories. To my mind, it is absurd to say that the rat isn't conscious of the tone and the shock. The rat is alive, awake, and remembering. What he doesn't possess is the highest level of human self-consciousness. He no doubt has some kind of me-ness, a subliminal sense of his own organism and its drives to fight, play, flee, have sex, and eat, and he surely recognizes his fellow rats and can distinguish them from predators. He does not have an internal narrator telling the story of his adventures in the lab with those gargantuan scientists in white coats delivering tones and unpleasant bursts of electricity.

Shaking looks like a fear response, one of "the somatic manifestations of anxiety." "He was trembling with fear" is a cliché. The sound of thunder would send the border collie of my childhood, Balder, running to his bed, where he would become a trembling lump of black-and-white fur. When I'm crossing the street and a car unexpectedly turns into the crosswalk, I always freeze momentarily before rushing out of the way, but even when I respond instantly, before I am fully aware of my fear and its object, I feel my heart beating and my lungs tighten. On the day my convulsions began, I had no awareness of either the object of my fear or the normal signs of fear. I felt the shaking but had no way to identify it *as anything*. I want to stress that at the time, rather stupidly, it never occurred to me that it would happen again. I was convinced that it was a singular event and, as such, I was able to regard it with fascination rather than alarm. Having to speak in public has become my tone or clap of thunder, and if there is a memory involved, it is implicit, not explicit, and the shaking itself doesn't involve my higher self-reflexive consciousness. But *talking* and *thinking* and staying calm do. In order to keep talking, despite my shaking, I have to use a part of my brain that can, in fact, regulate fear—the medial and ventral prefrontal cortex. LeDoux argues, "Pathological fear, then, may occur when the amygdala is unchecked by the prefrontal cortex, and treatment of pathologic fear may require that the patient learn to increase activity in the prefrontal region so that the amygdala is less free to express fear."[117] He further argues that the relation between the amygdala and the prefrontal region is reciprocal—that is, if one is turned on, the other is inhibited. But that is not what happened to me. I talked *and* shook, although in the end, some part of me seemed to be able to put a lid on the blasting alarm coming from down under. On the other hand, perhaps my feeling of control was an illusion.

In my case, two systems appear to be entirely cut off from each other initially, until the regulator takes hold. Still, as scientists like to say, correlation is not cause. Maybe the two things have nothing to do with each other. And why I shook the *first* time remains mysterious. The first event is significant, because neural networks are sensitive and, once formed, are prone to repetition. In neuroscience, one of the first ideas I learned, no doubt made memorable by the convenient rhyme, was Hebb's law: "Neurons that fire together wire together." The more I shake, the more likely it is that I'll shake in the future. Can I say that the shaking woman is a repeatedly activated pattern of firing neurons and stress hormones released in an involuntary response, which is then dampened as I keep my cool, continue to talk, convinced that I am not really in any danger? Is that all there is to the story?

In his book *The Astonishing Hypothesis,* Francis Crick, who, with James Watson, discovered DNA, explained his title: "You, your joys and your sorrows, your memories and your ambitions, your sense of personal identity and free will are, in fact, no more than the behaviour of a vast assembly of nerve cells and their associated molecules."[118] Crick may indeed be expressing a truth, but there's something wrong with his formulation nevertheless. Would anyone deny that Tolstoy's "The Death of Iván Ilých" is paper and ink or that Giorgione's *The Tempest* is canvas and paint? And yet, how far does that get us in expressing what these works are? Am I wrong in feeling that "a vast assembly of nerve cells" is an inadequate description of *me* or that those words fail to answer the question, What happened to me? Am I looking for a narrative, a confabulation, to interpret a debility that is no more and no less than synaptic wiring and firing? Joseph LeDoux is less of a reductionist than Crick. He acknowledges that there are levels of human reality. Revealingly, he puzzles over the question Freud asked in 1895, as he worked on his *Project*, the same question the conversion researchers asked, the two men who found themselves translating J. Russell Reynolds into updated language more than a century after his lecture. LeDoux writes, "The problem is that it is not clear how the changes at the neural level relate to those at the psychological level."[119] There's the rub.

LURIA'S S. SEEMED TO TRANSLATE all of his experience into visual form. I seem to translate everything into bodily feelings and sensations. Several years ago, I received a letter from a person who belongs to an international synesthesia organization. She had read my books and become convinced that I *had it*. My knowledge of the phenomenon was shallow at the time, and I wrote back saying that numbers and letters weren't colored for me and left it at that. What she didn't say is that there is something called mirror-touch synesthesia, which is when a person feels another person being touched or in pain simply by looking at him or her.[120] But then this form of synesthesia wasn't described or named until 2005. When I was a child, my mother used to tell me that I was "too sensitive for this world." She didn't mean it unkindly, but for many years I chalked up my hypersensitivity to a character flaw. For as long as I can remember, I have felt the taps, knocks, and bumps, as well as the moods, of other people, *almost* as if they are mine. I can tell the difference between an actual touch and the one I feel when I look, but the sensation is there nevertheless. I feel the sprained ankle of someone else as a pain in my own. Watching a mother caress a child gives me the physical pleasure I would give or take from the same gesture. If someone is being hurt in a movie, I must close my eyes or head for the exit. As a girl I spent half of every episode of *Lassie* in the bathroom. Violent movies and horror films are intolerable to me because I *feel* the victim's torture. Looking at or even thinking about ice or an ice cube makes me shiver. My empathy is extreme and, to be frank, I sometimes feel too much and need to protect myself from overexposure to stimuli that will turn me into a pillar of aching flesh. All of this is apparently typical of people with mirror-touch synesthesia.

I also have powerful *feeling* responses to colors and light. For example, during a trip to Iceland, I was in a bus looking out the window at that extraordinary treeless landscape when we passed a lake that had an unusual color. Its water was a glacially pale blue-green. The color assaulted me as if it were a shock. It ran up and down my whole body, and I found myself resisting it, closing my eyes, waving my hands in an effort to expel that intolerable hue from my body. My traveling companion, sitting beside me, asked me what was wrong. "I can't bear that color," I told her. "It hurts me." Understandably, she was surprised. Most people aren't attacked by colors. Various kinds of light create distinct emotions in me: the balm of afternoon sun through a window, the irritant of dim streetlights, the cruelty of fluorescence. Luria quotes S. as saying, "When I ride the trolley I can feel the clanging it makes in my teeth."[121] Noises often affect my teeth. A sound knocks them or burns in them or buzzes through my gums. Perhaps this is ordinary. I don't know. If I look at too many paintings (and I love paintings), I become dizzy and nauseated. This affliction also has a name: Stendhal syndrome. But in me, at least, it is related to migraine and can develop into a full-blown headache.

One may ask why this condition—or, rather, state of being—has only recently been identified. The answer, in part, is mirror neurons. One theory is that in people like me they are overactive. Without Gallese, Rizzolatti and their colleagues' discovery and the research that followed, my version of synesthesia would probably have remained unidentified in the world of hard science, a *psychological* state without an organic concomitant. Neurobiologists would have regarded it with skepticism (as they did all forms of synesthesia, until it became clear that it could be understood as a function of genetic and neural processes) or they simply would have ignored it as a subject beyond their ken. Without a biologically plausible hypothesis, a study is not possible. The wane of behaviorism in psychology has, no doubt, also played a role. Suddenly, subjective states, at least in some circles, have become a reasonable focus of study. Anglo-American analytical philosophers, writing in the *Journal of Consciousness Studies,* debate endlessly the problem of *qualia*—each person's phenomenal, personal experience of the world, which cannot (according to some) be reduced to a description of activated neuronal circuits or "information processing." There are scientists in various fields who would disagree with the reductionist formulation "You are a vast assembly of nerve cells."

Many people experience relief when they discover that a trait that has always been with them has a name, belongs to a legitimate scientific category, and is part of a greater taxonomy of illnesses and syndromes. In *Blue Cats and Chartreuse Kittens,* Patricia Lynne Duffy describes her happiness in 1975 when she came across an article in *Psychology Today* that described her color synesthesia. "I read it, wide-eyed, amazed to find that my offbeat 'visions' were part of a documented pattern of perception with a history and even a place in scientific literature."[122] Mirror-touch synesthesia is a newly minted phenomenon, supposedly rare. My feeling is now that it has been officially diagnosed, hordes of us may rush into the open in far larger numbers than researchers suspect. After all, the heart of this condition is empathy, and in human beings, empathy exists on a sliding scale from radical participation in the feelings of others to complete indifference. People with autism have great difficulty imagining the minds of others. Psychopaths, on the other hand, may brilliantly read people in order to manipulate them but notoriously lack all empathetic connection to their fellow human beings. Similarly, people who have sustained damage to the frontal lobes of their brains become strangely cold, utterly changed from their former selves, as is illustrated by the famous neurological case of the railroad foreman Phineas Gage, who survived a grotesque injury. After a steel beam passed through his frontal lobes, he appeared to have made a miraculous recovery. His personality, however, had changed. Once a mild-mannered, responsible person, Gage could no longer plan ahead. He became volatile and weirdly indifferent to others. Both guilt and empathy vanished with the pieces of his brain he lost in the accident.

DESPITE THE NEWNESS of mirror-touch synesthesia, a phenomenon known as *transitivism* has been around in neurology and psychology since Carl Wernicke first coined the term in 1900. The psychiatrist defined it as a projection of one's own symptoms onto a double to save the self.[123] The doppelgänger carries your suffering for you or acts out your wishes, as did S.'s "he." In psychiatry, the word is still used to describe a state in which patients (often psychotic) confuse themselves with another person. The threshold between the "I" and the "you" begins to merge or collapses entirely. Charlotte Buhler, a child psychologist born in Vienna in 1893, noticed that transitivism is common among young children. Lacan cites Buhler in his famous 1949 lecture on the mirror stage, but the phenomenon is familiar to most parents who have witnessed this scene on a playground: A toddler falls down and bursts into tears. A playmate nearby watches the fall and begins to cry. One is hurt; the other isn't—but both are bawling inconsolably. This is the mingling of transitivism.

K. Hitomi, a neuropsychiatrist in Osaka, Japan, writes about two schizophrenic patients in his paper " 'Transitional Subject' in Two Cases of Psychotherapy of Schizophrenia."[124]

His first patient was a woman in her thirties who became ill during adolescence and had not responded to drugs. The doctor brought a doll to therapy, whom the patient named T. It soon became clear that T served as an external object or double for the woman herself. Once, when the patient was crying and seemed unable to stop, her doctor asked, "Who is crying?" "It's me," she said. "How about T?" "Oh, T may cry, too, at times." Hitomi notes, "The patient blinked for a moment looking puzzled, but then she shouted, 'Oh, T began to cry,' and the patient did not cry any longer." As time went on, T took over more functions. The doppelgänger stood guard at night to ward off imagined attackers so the patient could sleep soundly. When the doll took a spill on the floor, her alter ego cried "Ouch!" Later T became a participant in the woman's regression to an infantile state, from which she emerged better.

The second patient became his therapist's reflection. After watching his physician straighten his tie, the sick man announced, "I am the mirror." In every session after that, he drew his psychotherapist, paying particular attention to the man's neckties, but over the course of a few months, these sketches began to change, to look more and more like the patient himself, until they became not an image of the other but a self-portrait.[125] Neither of these stories would come as a surprise to psychotherapists or to anyone who has spent time in a psychiatric ward. They are tales from the world of *Between*.

Hitomi's use of the term "transitional subject" refers to Winnicott's "transitional object." For Winnicott, transitional phenomena designate "the intermediate area" of human experience.[126] It was Winnicott who named and interpreted the ordinary need in children to hold their "blankeys" or bears or pacifiers or suck their thumbs or hear the same song every night before going to bed. He also understood that for a child the transitional object is a symbol of something else—his mother's breast or body or presence—but its great importance is also that it is a *real* thing *between* them. The first patient's doll wasn't an object so much as an alternative subject onto which she could project her fragile self and with which she could protect it. As the therapy progressed, the doll's role became less important, and the patient began to interact directly with the doctor, who metamorphosed into her mother. The man, on the other hand, became his therapist's reflection in order to find his own mirror image. He temporarily borrowed the stability of his physician.

His focus on the necktie interests me, because above the tie is the face, the locus of intimate interactions and the part of the body that figures most heavily in both recognition and identification—two distinct processes. *I know you. You're Fred.* (I've often wondered how well I would recognize the hands or feet of people I know. I'd have to know them pretty well.) Unless we are overcome with shyness, we speak to a person's face, especially to her eyes, because that is where we feel we can find her. What happens between two people, even in an ordinary conversation, isn't easily quantified or measured. Between the two interlocutors there is much that goes on that is not articulated. We are always reading faces, and numerous reflections, projections, transferences, and identifications take place at different levels of our awareness.

In the first case reported by Hitomi, the patient and therapist were able to use a doll as a transitional self-object between them to play with forms of her broken identity. In the second, the patient used the therapist as a mirror that would gradually reflect back himself. In both cases, doubling offered an avenue to healing. Alienation into another representative thing (the doll) or person (the therapist) helped restore the "self."

DURING THE LAST WEEK I spent with my father before he died, my mother and I followed a routine. We would often arrive in the afternoon to visit him because that was the time of day when he had more strength for talking. We left him in the evenings, after my mother helped him prepare for bed—performing the rituals of teeth brushing, moisturizing his dry skin, and making sure his pillows, sheets, and blanket were comfortably arranged. Then my mother and I would say good night to him, drive home, and usually go quickly to sleep. I think we were both emotionally exhausted, although we rarely mentioned it to each other. On one of those last nights, I crawled into the narrow, too short bed I had slept in as a child and pulled the covers over me. As I lay there, thinking of my father, I felt the oxygen line in my nostrils and its discomfort, the heaviness of my lame leg, from which a tumor had been removed years before, the pressure in my tightened lungs, and a sudden panicked helplessness that I could not move from the bed on my own but would have to call for help. For however long it lasted, only minutes, *I was my father*. The sensation was both overwhelming and awful. I felt the proximity of death, its inexorable pull, and I had to struggle to leap back into my own body, to find myself again.

I told my mother about my nighttime metamorphosis, and she said, "That's never happened to me." Of course, my mother had been taking care of my father for years as his emphysema worsened, and were she prone to such transformations, she would have been stopped in her tracks. By then, my father had given me permission to use his memoirs in the novel I was writing. When he died, I was already working on the book that was, in part, an imaginative version of his life. I had read and reread his memoir. I'd read the letters he had written to his parents when he was a soldier during the Second World War in the Pacific and, as an exercise, had typed those letters in order to feel them. Typing allowed his words to take on a physical reality beyond what I would have experienced by just reading them. My fingers can listen, too. I spent four and a half years writing the book. When I wrote the speech for the memorial, I paused from the novel, which was nearing its end, and had the strong sensation I wrote about earlier: as I planned the talk and wrote on my index cards, I felt his remembered voice. I suspect, although I cannot know, that when I opened my mouth to speak that day back home in Northfield, my identification with my father, always strong, had become even more intense. The words of the text I had written fell somewhere between us—not his, not quite mine—somewhere in the middle. One of the novel's dominant themes is traumatic memory. For the book, I borrowed my father's words, in which he tells about the murder of a Japanese officer, and recorded the passages he had written about his flashbacks, one in particular: a trembling fit he had as he listened to a hymn in the chapel on the St. Olaf College campus, not far from where I found myself the afternoon I shook so hard I thought I would fall down.

Here is a story. Is it a true story? It feels as if I am circling some emotional truth. *It still strikes me as strange that the case histories I write should read like short stories.* Freud was listening to stories. There are events, and we weave them into a narrative that makes some kind of sense. In his resonant essay "Mourning and Melancholia," Freud distinguishes between two forms of grief. The person in mourning, he argues, has suffered a conscious loss, and it is the outside world that turns gray and meaningless for the period of grieving. In melancholia, however, the afflicted person has powerful conflicted identifications with the dead person, some of which are unconscious, and the loss becomes internal, not external—a psychic wound.[127] Reading the essay again made me say to myself, Yes, there is something true here. And yet I don't suffer from the feelings of worthlessness Freud attributes to melancholics who berate themselves fiercely and seem utterly joyless. I am not depressed. There is, however, in my mourning a blur of betweenness or a partial possession by a beloved other that is ambivalent, complex, and heavily weighted with emotions I can't really articulate.

MY DAY: The paragraph above was the last thing I wrote after a few hours of work on a Tuesday morning, before I dashed off to have lunch at noon with a dear friend of mine, a psychiatrist and psychoanalyst. Among other things, we discussed finding me an analyst. I had decided to make the leap, and G. said he had a recommendation. When he told me this, I felt relieved. After lunch, I taught my two writing classes at the hospital as usual. In the first class, for adolescent patients, I had a single student, a sensitive, sober girl of sixteen who was also an eager writer. I'll call her D. Although I always ask my adult students to respond to a text, usually a poem, I have found that the young people do better with a single word, an emotional word. I chose *fear*. D. wrote about her fear of escalators, one she had successfully conquered. I wrote about my fear of being in cars, which had slowly begun to diminish. After that, I asked her if there was another emotion she'd like to address, and she said, "Sadness." In her essay, she wrote that she cuts herself. When she is sad, lonely, under pressure at school, or struggling with and sometimes failing tests, she cuts herself. Sadness and cutting go together. In the adult class, we read and responded to some poems by Theodore Roethke. Then I wandered around a bit in the city before I participated in a PEN event held at Cooper Union to promote the democratic cause of the monks in Burma. I took my propranolol and read aloud a short text written by a well-known Burmese comedian, Zargana, describing his brutal interrogation by the authorities after his first arrest, in 1988. He is now in

prison yet again for speaking out against the military government after the devastating Nargis storm. (I did not
shake.)

MY DREAM THAT NIGHT: I am wandering down corridors
and rooms and find myself in a lab of some kind, a small
barren place. A doctor in a white coat is standing there. He
tells me I have cancer. The number 3 is somehow part of his
diagnosis. The cancer is inoperable. I am dying. There is
nothing to be done, he says. I wander away from the physician, and it is only then that I become intensely aware of the
tumors under the skin at my throat and around my neck,
bulging protuberances that move under my fingers when I
touch them and that confirm my terminal state. Suddenly,
I am in the backseat of a moving car behind a Buddhist
monk in a saffron robe. Well, I think to myself, I've always
known that the book I am writing wouldn't be a long one,
but now I'll have to cut it short, end it sooner than I had expected. I'm dying. It will be the *last* book I write. This
makes me terribly sad—not desperate, as I would have been
in waking life, but unutterably, deeply sad. Then I woke up.

AS IS TRUE OF MANY DREAMS, this one collapsed my day
into a curious, dense little parable. Even before I crawled
out of bed, I understood that my dream tumors referred to
the malignant tumor the doctors removed from my father's
thigh, which left his leg stiff and useless, the leg I had felt so
intensely during my minutes of nearly complete identification with my father as I lay in my childhood bed. That my

cancerous tumors were popping out of my neck reminded me of Hitomi's schizophrenic patient who drew his therapist's ties until he began to focus on the features of a face, first his doctor's, then his own. The dream followed my day at the hospital, the day every week when I see psychiatrists in white coats come and go on the wards. That particular Tuesday at lunch G. had suggested a psychotherapist for me, and only hours before that, I had written about the importance of faces for recognizing and identifying other people. But the neck is also where the shaking woman begins. A sick neck served as the perfect dream image of my symptom: *From the chin up, I was my familiar self. From the neck down, I was a shuddering stranger.*

Isn't the neck the place where the head ends and the body begins? And isn't the mind/body conundrum, ambiguous though it may be, the subject of this book, the same book I am writing now and was writing in the dream and would have to cut short? My father's memoir was *his last book.* The number 3 hovers as the digit of gloom over the diagnosis— which summons Luria's S., also a character in this text, Mr. Synesthesia, visual-memory man par excellence, a person whose last initial is the same as my first. The car is a vehicle of fear. I had written about cars during my day at the hospital. Later that evening, I sat directly behind a Buddhist monk who had been a leader in the May 2008 demonstrations against the Burmese government and a figure like him then appears in the front seat of my dream automobile. Along with everyone else in the audience at Cooper Union, I had watched a film clip of demonstrators running from gunfire and wounded people bleeding in the streets of Rangoon. I had read the passage assigned to me. Near the end of his text, Zargana writes, "And yet, there was nothing we could do . . ." In the dream the physician said, "There is nothing to be done." My dream sadness looped back to D.'s sadness, to her cutting and to my *cutting short* the book—a sign perhaps of language cut short between me and my father, of last books, but also the voice, my voice in a lumpy diseased throat, and my father's voice, now silent, and my making speeches and trying to speak while I'm shaking, which is my symptom, my limp or lameness, transformed into a terminal illness in the dream, like my father's terminal illness, which was not in his leg but in his lungs and breath and which took his voice, a shaking, terrible silence—speechlessness.[128] When I last spoke to him on the telephone, he could no longer speak. Identification as psychic wound. And finally, the dream returned to one of the poems by Theodore Roethke I had read with the adult patients at Payne Whitney. Entitled "Silence," it ends with these lines:

> If I should ever seek relief
> From that monotony of grief,
> The tight nerves leading to the throat
> Would not release one riven note:
> What shakes my skull to disrepair
> Shall never touch another ear.[129]

IN THE *INTERPRETATION OF DREAMS*, Freud writes, "I have already had occasion to point out that it is in fact never possible to be sure that a dream has been completely interpreted. Even if the solution seems satisfactory and without gaps the possibility remains that the dream may have yet another meaning."[130] Meaning is something we find and make. It is never complete. There are always holes. There is no consensus among scientists about why we sleep or why we dream. Nobody knows for sure. Sleep researchers agree that what Freud called *Tagereste*, translated as the "day residue," shows up in our dreams. Many, not all, agree that dreams are often more emotional than waking life. It is known that the executive portions of the brain that inhibit our actions when we're awake (the dorsolateral prefrontal cortex) are largely dormant when we sleep and dream. There has long been an idea among some scientists that sleep helps solidify memories, but others disagree. There is no consensus that dreams *mean* anything. Scientists are divided about exactly what parts of the brain are active and inactive; those who agree, often interpret the activity in different ways. In opposition to earlier orthodoxy, it is now known that there are REM dreams and non-REM dreams. The once direct association between rapid eye movement and dreaming no longer holds. A number of researchers have asserted that dreams are a kind of chaotic discharge, a churning nocturnal garbage dump that involves no higher-order functions, that dreams, by their very nature, cannot hold or reveal complex ideas. Among the most prominent dream researchers is Allan Hobson, a vigorous anti-Freudian, who proposed the activation-synthesis theory of dreaming. This theory maintains that the pontine brain stem, part of the old brain, in evolutionary terms, is critical to dreaming. According to Hobson and his colleague Robert McCarley, dreams have "no primary ideational, volitional, or emotional content."[131] Hobson has further insisted that dream plots have no coherent order and do not involve self-reflexive awareness. In one experiment, he took dream reports, cut them into pieces, and asked people to reassemble them in the correct order, something that turned out to be very hard to do.[132]

But using my own dream as an example, I have to ask, Wouldn't the doctor's diagnosis of my cancer have to precede my pondering that same diagnosis in the car? Isn't that a form of story logic? Didn't my dreaming mind manufacture a narrative of my encounter with fatal news followed by my sadness about it? And although I didn't know I was dreaming, doesn't my dream self have a form of self-reflexive awareness? Didn't that self meditate on last books and the end of life? And doesn't the dream contain condensed ideas and primary emotional content? Am I a singular dreamer, someone without precedent in the history of the world? I doubt it. This is a case where a working theory leaves out the cases that run counter to it.

An article on the subject by Antti Revonsuo nods to Freud in its title, "The Reinterpretation of Dreams: An Evolutionary Hypothesis of the Function of Dreaming." Unlike some researchers, Revonsuo cites the "overwhelming evidence" that dream content reflects the "emotional problems of the dreamer."[133] My dream appears to be a potent illustration of that truth. In order to make an evolutionary argument that dreaming is an older function of the brain, however, that our conflicted dreams are a kind of training ground of the mind to prepare us to face threats, he writes, "Therefore the principal reason we do not dream about writing, reading and doing arithmetic probably is that all these are cultural latecomers that have to be hammered into our cognitive architecture."[134] Following Revonsuo's hypothesis, I am a more evolved creature than most other human beings because *I dream about writing and reading all the time.* As flattering as it might be to think of myself as further along on the evolutionary scale, this idea strikes me as dubious. Typing at my computer, reading books, finding letters and other texts, as well as hearing significant, often seemingly revelatory words have long played an important role in my dream life. Whatever one may think of my powers as a dream interpreter, my cancer dream served, among other things, as an answer to my having read Roethke's "Silence" earlier that day. Until I reread the poem again *after* the dream, I had not noticed the striking relevance of the words for me personally: not just *relief, grief,* and *throat* but *shakes.* Without any acknowledgment from that fully awake teacher in the classroom, another part of me took in the poet's language and respun it in the dream.

My daily writing and reading are often transmuted into a dream language or logic when I sleep. A friend of mine, R., a physicist who is now involved in neuroscience research on perception, related a dream to me while we were having lunch. I asked him to retell the story in an e-mail:

I had been working for days on a complicated calculation that required many pages of intricate algebra, with two central mathematical quantities that played a symmetrical role. I named them x and x prime. As a whole, the problem resisted me; whenever I had the feeling I was nearing a resolution, the calculation lashed back at me. One night, I dreamt of two twin brothers. Brash, unpleasant, aggressive, the two had come from some distant country. They were both human actors in the dream, but at the same time I knew they were x and x prime. I clearly remember my impression during the dream that these were the elements of my calculation and that they were manifestly antagonistic to my will. At first they behaved in a contained manner, then became more erratic. As far as I can remember, over the course of the dream, they progressively became less identified with x and x prime and more truly human.

As you can see, it was not that I was carrying out the calculation proper in my dream, but that some of the elements had taken human form, and although they could not be manipulated algebraically, they had retained the "character" they had in the calculation.

Several times I have woken up (in the morning or in the middle of the night) to a clear mathematical conclusion, as if I had done the calculation in detail in my sleep. I could just go to a piece of paper and write it down, all crisp in my head.

R.'s dream of the x twins looks remarkably like S.'s waking world of numbers with swollen feet or temperaments of gloom and cheer. S. lived in an ongoing dream of vivid concrete personifications and images. It's as if his dream machinery never shut off. After a night's sleep, R. has sometimes solved mathematical problems, just as I have often woken to find a way out of a writing impasse—the solution appeared to have been given to me during the night. No doubt, R. and I have powerful emotional attachments to our work, which then make their way into our dreamscapes. At the very least, however, I have unearthed two examples of people who have dreams that feature transformations of written texts and mathematical formulations. Arguably, R. and I are still working in our sleep.

But who is the dreamer in the dream, the "I" that walks and talks and rides around in cars at night? Is it the "I" of daylight? Is it another "I"? Does that hallucinating nocturnal being have anything useful to tell me? Dreams are a part of our consciousness but not our waking consciousness. The continual stimuli that bombard us during the day are missing at night, and the mind manufactures its own hallucinatory material, at least in part as compensation for what has disappeared. The transitions in dreams are often violent—I don't know how I climbed into that car with the monk, for example. The laws of physics do not apply in that parallel world. And dreams are less abstract than wakeful thoughts: the signs of a day's work, x and x prime, are transformed into belligerent brothers at night. Neck tumors succinctly condense my worries to a single nocturnal image. But could I be wrong? Is there really anything meaningful about dreams? Is my reading of a dream just my left-brain interpreter churning away the morning after, imposing a narrative on what are mere fragments? No, I don't believe that. It seems to me that dreaming is *another form of thinking,* more concrete, more economical, more visual, and often more emotional than the thoughts of the day, but a *thinking through* of the day, nevertheless. And even if I've changed sex or grown fur or am flying through the air, the first-person pronoun belongs to me in the dream, my dreaming "I."

My intuition that dreams are not nonsense, arrived at through my own experiences during sleep, is not without its scientific advocates. Having studied people with neurological lesions that change their dreaming patterns, Mark Solms disputes that dreams are mere mental junk. He writes, "It appears that *specific forebrain mechanisms are involved in the generation of dream imagery* and that *this imagery is actively constructed through complex cognitive processes.*"[135] In other words, some higher mental functions are active during dreaming. Intellectual melees continue to be waged over this issue, with strong proponents on both sides. In 2006, Hobson and Solms staged a formal debate in Tuscon, hosted by the Center for Consciousness Studies. The issue was Freud's dream theory: Solms for, Hobson against. Although Hobson has modified his earlier belief that dreams are without any significance and are symbol-free, he lost the debate to Solms (the audience voted) by a large margin.[136] I continue to be fascinated by how controversial Freud remains and how emotional the discussions surrounding his ideas are. My own view is that conceding Freud was right about some aspects of the mind does not mean he wasn't wrong about others. Is there any reason to insist on embracing or rejecting a theory as a whole?

As far as I can tell, the idea that dreams have both form and meaning has grown among researchers. Whatever the case may be, my own inner life was affected by my dream, with its strange but concise components. And perhaps most of all, the dream left me with the trace of an emotion that genuinely reflects my trouble. If I discovered tomorrow that I had inoperable cancer, I would not just feel sad, I would be terrified, mutinous, devastated. In the dream I was only sad, strangely deliberate, resigned, and capable of calm meditation on my lot. In other words, it was a dream not about my own death but about my relation to another death—one I seem to be carrying around with me every day like a disease. I may be wrong, but I feel I've never been as close to the shaking woman as in that dream.

THESE QUESTIONS RETURN US to the problem of subjective experience. Dreams use the language and imagery of waking life, but their meanings are personal. Like most contemporary psychoanalysts, I do not believe in universal dream symbols, that stairs signify one thing and trees or kites another. Dreams are stories made by and for the dreamer, and each dreamer has his own folds to open and knots to untie. Had I not unraveled my dream through the events of my day and the driving emotions of my present life, it surely would have read as nonsense. To exclude complex subjective reality from dream research strikes me as myopic. Close attention to the dreamer's day life doesn't make a dream report less disjointed or bizarre; it renders those same qualities significant by placing them in a broader context. Nevertheless, there is no objective reading of a dream. Is this the character of interpretation in general? It is no secret that our personal experiences infect our ideas about how the world works. If Antti Revonsuo were scribbling or calculating regularly in his own dreams, it is doubtful he would have advanced the idea that these activities are missing from everyone's nighttime hallucinations. It is certainly possible that most people are not typing and doing sums in their sleep. My friend R.'s calculation did not involve manipulating algebra but instead personified its symbols. I often type in my dreams but can rarely remember what I am writing. Nevertheless, we appear as exceptions to Revonsuo's hypothesis, and exceptions must also find their way into a theoretical account of human dream life. The truth is that personality inevitably bleeds into all forms of our intellectual life. We all extrapolate from our own lives in order to understand the world. In art, this is considered an advantage; in science, a contamination.

A dramatic example of an overlap between the personal and the intellectual occurred at a lecture I attended. Among other topics, the presenter spoke about neuroscience and its uses for psychotherapy. She also spent some time talking about empathy and the brain. During the question-and-answer session, a man in the back of the room stood up and announced that he was an engineer who was also immersed in brain studies. He then demonstrated some of his knowledge, the content of which I don't remember, but it was plain he was no fool. Then he stated loudly and forcefully that empathy does not exist. The very idea was preposterous. He did not believe in it. The room, filled with a couple hundred people, mostly psychotherapists and psychiatrists, was silent. But I had a potent sensation of a current running through the audience like an inaudible murmur, if such a thing is possible. Politely, silently, a mass diagnosis was taking place, one that, I confess, flashed immediately through my own head: Asperger's.

Surely, it is difficult to believe in an emotional state you never experience. It is not like believing in Antarctica or neurons or quarks. Even if one has no personal knowledge of these entities, has never actually *seen* them, they may be taken on faith, part of our intersubjective cultural knowledge. In contrast, the world of our feelings is so internal, so inseparable from being itself that every notion we entertain about normality becomes highly subjective. To argue that the man at the back of the room has a "condition," currently a fashionable diagnosis, that makes him *abnormal* does not detract from my point: it is often difficult to untangle personality and feeling states from belief systems, ideas, and theories.

In *Pragmatism,* William James makes a distinction between "tough-minded" and "tender-minded" philosophers, arguing that the two are temperamentally at odds. "The tough think of the tender as sentimentalists and softheads. The tender feel the tough to be unrefined, callous, or brutal."[137] As a pluralist, James will locate Pragmatism between the two, but the division he made remains valuable. Despite the looseness of these categories, they remind us of an ongoing division between styles of thought. (James, conciliatory in tone, nevertheless firmly believed that thought devoid of feeling was perverse.)

For a long time, I read only modern European philosophers and ignored the Americans and the English. When I got around to reading Anglo-American analytical philosophers, I found myself on a new planet. The Analyticals, as I call them, like to put forth truth conditions and logico-mathematical formulas that explain the way things are, as if the shifting stream of life is a game of true and false and human experience belongs to no one. They are fond of thought experiments that feature zombies (they look and act just like us but don't have consciousness). They also tell and retell the story of Mary, the brilliant neuroscientist who lives in a black-and-white box and knows all there is to know about color and the brain. One day, she leaves her box and sees a red flower. Does she see anything new? These games are not meant to be about the actual world or our living in it. They are meant to make us think abstractly about a philosophical problem. I know it is cheating to say I *feel* that another person isn't a zombie when I sit across from him in a room and look into his eyes, and it is probably also cheating to wonder how color deprivation for all those years would have changed both Mary's brain and her personality, so that by the time she left her room, it might be hard to know *what* she would see in terms of color and, furthermore, if she had a brain like mine, would she then know that she had to shun a particular shade of turquoise? And what does knowing *all there is to know* mean? Does it mean knowledge from books? Does it include the fact that color acts on us pre-consciously before we're able even to name the color we're seeing?[138]

These philosophers are the men and women (more men than women) of *Kiesewetter's Logic,* the schoolbook Iván Ilých returns to in his mind during the last days of his life. They do not all agree about Mary's experience of red or about the nature of consciousness. They quarrel loudly among themselves, and I am drawn far more to the ideas of some than of others. The philosopher Ned Block, for example, has found himself increasingly interested in the mysteries of neu-rological illnesses as he wrestles with a biological theory of consciousness. Unlike Daniel Dennett, who does not believe in qualia,[139] Block takes phenomenal experience seriously and does not think it can be explained away. In an interview, he speculated that philosophers who do not "appreciate" phe-nomenology may, like the poet-translator I met, lack the abil-ity to produce visual imagery, a thought that echoes my own about the engineer who refused to accept that empathy ex-ists.[140] William James, however, would no doubt have put all the Analyticals in the "tough-minded" camp. I am not op-posed to reason or logic. It is the ground for consensus in most disciplines, essential to our collective conversations, and it is not that I am unimpressed with these writers or even that they are always uncompelling but, rather, that when I read them, I often feel a chill.

Every once in a while, that coolness turns ice-cold. Peter

Carruthers, an Oxford-trained philosopher, defines consciousness as the ability to have second-order beliefs—that is, to be able not only to have experience A but to know that you are having experience A. The consequence of this idea is that if animals cannot do this, they are unconscious.

> Similarly then in the case of brutes: since their experiences, including their pains, are nonconscious ones, their pains are of no immediate moral concern. Indeed, since all the mental states of brutes are nonconscious, their injuries are lacking in even indirect moral concern.[141]

Carruthers's thinking is nothing if not logical. Once the first idea is accepted, the second follows. While some of us may wonder why animals who learn to avoid painful stimuli in a laboratory should be thought of as *unconscious* or ask, further, why pain would be significant only when it can be reflected upon or represented—*Gosh that hurts. I am having pain*—this is outside Carruthers's argument. For Carruthers, "consciousness" occupies the same position "spirit" did for the seventeenth-century occasionalist philosopher Malebranche. This Cartesian thinker believed that because animals had no souls and only through our souls and God were human beings able to experience mental states, it followed that our purely material animal cousins could not experience pain. It seems to me that Carruthers has confused consciousness with self-consciousness. In all events, his impeccable reasoning demonstrates how a single logical step can result in what, for me, is a repugnant and wrongheaded idea.

Perhaps I am hopelessly tender-minded, but can logical formulations encompass *everything*? As Ludwig Wittgenstein famously wrote near the end of his supremely logical *Tractatus Logico-philosophicus*:

> 6.521 The solution of the problem of life is seen in the vanishing of the problem. (Is this not the reason why those who have found after a long period of doubt that the sense of life became clear to them have then been unable to say what constituted that sense?)

> 6.522 There are, indeed, things that cannot be put into words. They *make themselves manifest*. They are what is mystical. . . .
> What we cannot speak about we must pass over in silence.[142]

Wittgenstein wrote the *Tractatus* during the period when he was a soldier at the front during the First World War. I do not find it strange that he found it necessary to allow for that which is wordless, the unsymbolized, unsystemized, uncontained—that which escapes us. I have never been able to believe that any system, no matter how seductive, can hold the ambiguities that are inherent in being a person in the world. Wittgenstein thought he had solved the problems of philosophy in the *Tractatus* (although there were "things" that remained forever outside the discipline's grasp). He changed his mind. The man of the *Tractatus* was not identical to the man of the later *Philosophical Investigations*. From a logical position, *What does Caius have to do with little Ványa?* is a question with an obvious answer: Caius and Ványa are both human beings. Human beings are mortal, and so both Caius and Ványa will die. From another point of view, however, this is wrong, because the irrational answer strikes at the core of what it means to be human. *The reality of little Ványa does not admit death* is not a mad proposition. Does the gap between the two represent the chasm between an objective perspective and a subjective one, between science, with its necessary logic, and art, with its private irrationality, between Husserl's *Körper* and *Leib*?

In her review of Merleau-Ponty's *The Phenomenology of Perception* in 1945, Simone de Beauvoir eloquently protests the dictates of science that dominate the education of children, and that ask a child to "renounce his subjectivity":

> Science enjoins him to escape out of his own consciousness, to turn away from the living and meaningful world that this consciousness disclosed to him, and for which science tries to substitute a universe of frozen objects, independent of all gaze and all thought.[143]

Beauvoir is right that much of science (as well as much of analytical philosophy) proceeds from an anonymous third-person view of a paralyzed world, which can then be broken down into legible truths. For Francis Crick and a philosopher such as Patricia Churchland, the mind is neurons.[144] It is no more or less. When we fully uncover the anatomy of the brain and its functions, the story will be told, completely. There are more nuanced positions than these. Maybe mind *emerges* from the brain, as some argue, echoing La Mettrie in *L'Homme Machine*. Or might the problem simply be a matter of your point of view? Inside my head, the world feels immediate. I look out at people and things in all their variety. I think and laugh and cry, but when you open up my skull and peek inside, all you see in there are two connected clumps of gray and white matter. And, if I am asleep, you don't see my dreams. There are those who speculate that some form of consciousness is not limited to human beings and animals but goes all the way down to the deepest levels of the universe. Some cognitive scientists, such as Francisco Varela, and other theoreticians have drawn insights from Buddhism and various mystical practices to gain insight into a selfless reality.[145] Others believe that there is a pan-psychic oneness.[146] Some scientists—physicists, in particular—have left the idea of substance far behind them and delved into the curious regions of quantum theory. They are not guilty of freezing objects or leaving out the role of the observer on the observed. Apparently, in quantum field theory there are states that are seen by one person as a vacuum and by another as a mixture of particles. I have no real understanding of how this works, but I take the physicists at their word. What is seen depends on the perspective of the seer.

The theoretical physicist Jan-Markus Schwindt, a latter-day idealist, turns Crick on his head: "I do not think that mind exists in the physical world," he writes. "I rather think that the physical world exists within mind."[147] This thought is identical to the eighteenth-century philosopher George Berkeley's declaration that "all the choir of heaven and furniture of the earth, in a word, all those bodies which compose the mighty frame of the world, have not any subsistence without a mind."[148] And what is *mind* for Schwindt? "Mind consists of a conscious observing and an unconscious processing unit, like in a dream." His proposal for a new scientific model echoes Beauvoir's passage. It should, he writes, "take the role of the subject much more seriously than in present science which is a science of objects."[149] Schwindt is thinking not only through the lens of physics but more broadly through philosophy. Although he does not mention Berkeley, he cites both Schopenhauer and Husserl in his paper. The latter's phenomenology was essential to Merleau-Ponty, whose book Beauvoir reviewed. She, in turn, was influenced by both Husserl and Merleau-Ponty.

Ideas are infectious, and they shape us. But how do we end up choosing among them? Isn't it likely that our unempathetic engineer found the mechanistic models of his field amenable to his tough-minded personality? This, of course, doesn't make his working models ineffective or wrong; but it may make other perspectives less attractive, even less comprehensible. Someone like Schwindt is used to thinking big, or small, depending on how you look at it. The notion that everything is mind doesn't threaten him. He finds it congenial. Perhaps this is to be expected from someone who has grown accustomed to contemplating wave functions in "Hilbert spaces" or the even more uncanny "Minkowski space." And Schwindt is by no means alone. A number of his fellow physicists believe that it is consciousness that produces physical reality, rather than the other way around. With thinkers like these, the categories tough- and tender-minded no longer seem to apply.

Imants Baruss, a psychology professor at the University of Western Ontario, conducted a study on personality and belief in 2006. He and his fellow workers produced a complex personality test, that also allowed them to profile each subject's ideas about the character of reality, and then they correlated the results. They had expected to find the classic split between those who believe in a purely physical world, founded on the principles of a material science, and those with religious beliefs who embrace dualism, a universe made of both spirit and matter. What they hadn't expected to find was a third category, which they called "extraordinary transcendence." The people in this group were more likely to have had mystical or out-of-body experiences, to eschew conventional religion, and, like Schwindt, to agree with the supposition that everything is mental. They scored higher on tests for both openness and intelligence. To what degree this research reflects a broad public is anybody's guess. But one small finding caught my attention. As part of IQ evaluations, the subjects were asked to identify objects from a scrambled image. They had to re-assemble a thing in their minds that had been broken into pieces. Baruss comments, "Those who are better able to mentally synthesize visual fragments into a whole picture are more likely to believe that there is more to reality than meets the eye."[150] I would elaborate: maybe people who can integrate fragments and form a unified picture are people who understand reality as not just a sea of *frozen material objects,* already given to us, but as a puzzle of perceptions that depends on the viewer.

Many of us, perhaps most often as children, have wondered what it would be like to be another person, to leap out of one mind into another. Of course, to compare minds, I would have to retain an awareness of what it feels like to be me in comparison to being you. Were I you and myself at the same time, would I feel a shock? Would I say, This is *so* different? What if I could experience the engineer's internal life? What if I could leap into Dr. Schwindt and understand quantum theory in a flash? What if I jumped into the poet-translator I met on that panel years ago, the man who remembers the words in novels, not the people, and read the way he does. How would the novels I have loved feel then?

The closest we can get to this entrance into another person's mind is through reading. Reading is the mental arena where different thought styles, tough and tender, and the ideas generated by them become most apparent. We have access to a stranger's internal narrator. Reading, after all, is a way of living inside another person's words. His or her voice becomes my narrator for the duration. Of course, I retain my own critical faculties, pausing to say to myself, *Yes, he's right about that* or *No, he's forgotten this point entirely* or *That's a clichéd character,* but the more compelling the voice on the page is, the more I lose my own. I am seduced and give myself up to the other person's words. Moreover, I am often lured in by very different points of view. The more alien, inhospitable, or difficult the voice, however, the more I find myself divided, occupying two heads at once. Overcoming resistance is one of the pleasures of reading. Some texts are forbiddingly hard to read, and when a light suddenly shines on an obscure passage, understanding it (or feeling that I've understood it) brings happiness.

But prejudice also plays an important role in reading. An idea about what a book is can be blinding. It is not hard to see why labels such as "classic," "Nobel Prize winner," or "best seller" sway readers. A person in one discipline may assiduously avoid the work of people in another. A neuroscientist told me that he had mentioned Freud in a lecture once and had taken "a lot of flak for it." Similarly, some psychoanalysts refuse to admit that neurobiology is important for their practices or they talk about egos and ids and superegos as if they were actual organs of the body, rather than concepts that allow us to imagine the workings of the mind. Continental philosophers often stay clear of Analyticals on the other side of the channel, and the other way around. We feed our beliefs and biases. Over and over in my travels as a writer I have been met with these sentences: "I don't read fiction, but my wife does. Could you sign the book to her?" The not-so-subtle underlying message is that masculinity aligns itself with nonfiction, while femininity is associated with frivolous "made-up" stories. Real men like *objective* texts, not the *subjective* wanderings of mere fiction writers, especially female ones, whose prose, whatever its character, is tainted by their sex before a single word has been read. This absurd notion is hardly universal, but none of us is untouched by bias, predilection, taste, a preference for one metaphor over another or long-held associations so ingrained that they are wholly unconscious or barely conscious. During much of the twentieth century, hordes of scientists were so alarmed by the notions of "subjective reports" and "introspection" that the very idea of mental visualization, much less synesthesia, was regarded as very possibly a fiction.

Perhaps the most famous example was the behaviorist J. B. Watson, who rejected mental imagery altogether, claiming it did not exist. Watson defended his position in a public debate at the Psychology Club in Washington, D.C., where he declared that "there has never been a discovery in subjective psychology; there has only been medieval speculation."[151] The year before that public dispute took place, Freud published *The Ego and the Id* (or "The I and the It"), in which he altered his earlier model of the mind. His three earlier categories, conscious, unconscious, and preconscious, first elaborated in *The Interpretation of Dreams*, were abandoned for a new approach based on how each new division of the mind functioned. Freud's concept of the ego, or I (*Ich*), was not the internal narrator or waking perceptual consciousness, with its myriad images. It included a developing bodily sense of a self, very similar to a body schema—which determines our feeling of separateness from other people—as well as completely unconscious processes. The id, or it (*das es*), was the wholly unconscious, timeless place of primal urges or drives. The superego, or "over I" (*über-Ich*), was similar to a personal conscience that came about through a person's first and most important identifications—with his parents. So at the time Freud was remapping his model of the mind with large regions of unconsciousness, Watson was denying that visual imagery, an everyday conscious experience for most people, even existed.

Ideas grow, but they often grow in deep and narrow ditches. Watson was a radical and controversial advocate of behaviorism, but his ideas have had far-reaching effects on science and the philosophy of science. There are people in the world who lack the ability to form images in their minds (my poet-translator and some philosophers perhaps), but they are a minority, and some of them are neurological patients. My question is, If Watson or his like-minded fellow scientists were seeing novels or remembering houses and landscapes or even the words of a text they had read by viewing them again in their minds on page 78, how could they question the existence of mental imagery? Moreover, doesn't everybody dream? Aren't dreams visual mental images? Dogmas can make people blind.

REPORT: JUNE 23, 2008. I am traveling with my husband and a friend. We are spending three days in the Pyrenees together and plan to take a walk in the mountains. J. has found one identified as "moderate" in his guide book that evaluates activities for tourists of varying degrees of prowess. We drive to the place where the walk begins, and I climb up the rocky mountain path, bounding from one stone to another. I am proud of my strength (showing off, if it must be told, for the two men behind me), and then I tire. Breathless, I sit down on a boulder and feel my body go into full-blown convulsions, which then subside. This is not emotional, I think to myself. This is not about my father's death. This is not conversion disorder. I say nothing to my husband or friend, who were too far away to witness my seizure. When I walk back down the mountain, I go slowly. The event has left me weak and unsteady. Later, I look back at a journal entry from that day and read, "I know it wasn't psychogenic. It was the exertion. It makes me wonder about my whole theory—there is something else going on. Could it be related to my peripheral neuropathy? Can that turn into the shakes?"

When I was in my thirties, I acquired a "body electric," to borrow Whitman's phrase. My arms and legs tingled. Shocks of varying degrees leapt up and down my limbs and face. For several months I ignored it. Then I began to fear that I was coming down with some debilitating neurological disease, such as multiple sclerosis. I went to my doctor, who quickly reassured me that MS did not present itself in this way. He called what I had peripheral neuropathy. I suspected that the culprit might be a drug I had been taking as a prophylactic against urinary tract infections. My doctor was doubtful, but when he consulted the *Physicians' Desk Reference,* neuropathy was among the possible side effects. The truth is that many drugs are connected to this symptom, which means that it's possible macrodantin was behind my electric nerves, and it is possible that it wasn't. I wondered aloud in the doctor's office if migraineurs might not be more vulnerable to these odd sensations than others, but Dr. K. said no. Later, I discovered that he was wrong. Tinglings and shocks and all manner of peculiar sensations—*paresthesias*—are common among chronic migraine patients. After undergoing a test for nerve damage, I was told I had the nerves of a sixty-year-old woman, and when I asked the neurologist for a prognosis, he soberly declared, "It could get better; it could get worse; it could stay the same." I burst out laughing. He did not see the joke. As it turns out, he was right on all counts. It gets better for a while; then it gets worse; and sometimes it stays the same for weeks on end.

MY FANTASY STORY about the shaking woman doubles back on itself as, one by one, living persons replace my imaginary doctors. On G.'s recommendation, I find myself sitting across from Dr. C., a psychiatrist and psychoanalyst, in her office on Park Avenue. Unlike my phantom analyst, Dr. C. is a woman. Like my figment, she has a kind and intelligent face. She listens patiently as I tell her the story of my shaking. When I suggest conversion disorder, she shakes her head gently, a rather sad smile on her face. She does not believe I am hysterical. And when I mention at some point that I had febrile convulsions as an infant, she is all attention. On the day of my christening, my fever rose to 106, and I went into convulsions that terrified my mother. I can't remember when I first heard my mother tell the story. Why did I mention it to Dr. C.? Because I was telling the fast version of my life story. Why haven't I written about it here? I missed it. I repressed it. She gives me the telephone number of Dr. L., a neurologist she knows and likes, someone with a reputation for humane treatment of patients, and I agree to make an appointment and have my nerves properly investigated.

DR. L. FAXES ME a ten-page questionnaire about my history. She includes a blank page for further comments. I write two single-spaced pages, documenting my shakes, my migraines, their auras, the tingling in my arms and legs—in short, everything I can think of that seems related to my nervous system. After I finish writing, I remember my room in the neurology ward at Mount Sinai Hospital. I can see the dirty roofs of buildings through the window, the beige tray table, and the small television, which in my memory is black and white, but this dubious detail probably tells more about my emotional state at the time than what I was actually seeing. *Nicholas Nickleby* is on TV, but the people on the screen are tiny and far away. I can't focus on them because I seem to be wrapped in layer upon layer of gauze. The thickness of Thorazine. The world has become remote, and I feel I would have to travel a long way to recover its immediacy, its aliveness, its color. I suddenly wonder if when I dragged myself out of bed in the hospital room all those years ago to make my way to the bathroom, I looked like the heavily sedated mental patients I work with every week, the people who shuffle, rather than walk, into the room, their limbs as stiff and wooden as marionettes'. I probably did. Those eight long days. The brusque, indifferent nurses. The interns with their smiles and pin pricks and questions. Is the memory of the hospital the reason why I canceled the epilepsy specialist?

THE DOCTOR IS TALL, forthright, articulate, and friendly. I like her broad, loose movements and feel I am in the presence of a confident person at ease in her body. She seems prepared to take her time. I can tell she has a slightly amused attitude toward my confession, which she has on her desk beside her—much of it gone over with a transparent blue marker. My guess is that she reads with the marker, that the motion of her hand is part of the way she absorbs information. I feel stupidly gratified that my case doesn't appear to bore her. I am not a cut-and-dried example of anything, it seems. After a short time, it is obvious that just as Dr. C. did, Dr. L. dismisses conversion disorder. She clearly regards it as absurd. She explains that I am *too old*. If I were fourteen she might entertain the thought, but at fifty-three it's not possible. I'm not sure this is strictly true as I think over the cases I've read about, but then again, my speculative self-diagnosis already took a hit on that climb in the Pyrenees. Also, I've begun to feel a tremor running through my limbs, not constantly, but often, as if the grand spasms are an exaggerated version of this buzz saw inside me. She, too, is interested in my febrile convulsions and declares that many people with seizures of one kind or another had them in the first six months of their lives.

I undress, put on a hospital gown, and walk back and forth across the room for her. We play clapping games. I touch my nose with my index finger. She looks in my eyes.

No sign of pressure or brain tumor. She strokes my hands and the bottom of my feet with a cold instrument. I feel it all. Good sign. She uses a tuning fork. She tells me I have "nice, fat arteries," and I'm pleased to hear this. She wants to know if I've ever taken Depakote for my migraines, an anti-seizure medicine. I tell her no. She recommends MRI, two of them.

I look at the sheet on which she has scrawled in a large but clear hand:

1. Please do Brain MRI: Temporal Lobe Epilepsy— without GADO. protocol 345.4
2. Cervical spine MRI—Nogado/posterior column, C-2— C-5. Dx323.9 / 721.1 Thank you. L.L. MD.

On the subway traveling home, I feel my mood, which had been buoyant with the doctor, drop precipitously. Dr. C. and Dr. L. have both been more than competent and extremely kind, but I understand that by debunking hysteria they have raised the specter of additional neurological illness, the possibility that I have more-than-just-migraine. While neither conversion disorder nor migraine is appealing as a diagnosis, neither one is fatal. Since my seizure in Paris in 1982, I have worried that my headaches may hover close to epilepsy. According to the authors of *Behavioral Aspects of Epilepsy,* "Migraine and epilepsy are in many respects similar brain disorders. Both are common. Epilepsy may be, and migraine is, by definition, a primary, presumably genetic disorder."[152] Later in the same chapter, they write, "The two disorders are more than twice as likely to occur in the same person."[153] In his book *Migraine,* Oliver Sacks reflects on the historical distinctions and overlaps between the two illnesses. Although there may be a theoretical relation between them, "in practice," he writes, "it is easy to differentiate migraines from epilepsies in the vast majority of cases." After listing the features that make a categorical diagnosis relatively simple, he acknowledges a "twilight region" that confounds "rigid nosologies." He then cites an author who coined the term "migralepsy" for a patient who showed symptoms of both.[154] I would place Dr. Sacks firmly in James's category of the tender-minded. Unlike many of his fellow practitioners, he acknowledges not only the twists and turns of medical history but the genuine ambiguities that arise when we try to attach names to phenomena that resist clarity: "Finally the problem may cease to be one of clinical or physiological differentiation, and become one of semantic decision: we cannot name what we cannot individuate."[155] Blurring borders create abiding conundrums.

SINCE CHILDHOOD I HAVE EXPERIENCED lifting sensations and euphorias, floods of deep feeling that arrive in my body as a lightness in my head and seem to pull me upward. An unearthly clarity of vision and a feeling of high, perfect joy have preceded my most brutal and durable headaches. And once, well into my adulthood, I saw my small pink man and his pink ox on the floor of my bedroom. Later, I discovered that apparitions of little figures also have a name: Lilliputian hallucinations. I now recognize all of these states as aura phenomena, part of my life as a migraineur. What has changed since I was a child are not the auras but the content I assign to them. I no longer imagine the presence of the supernatural. I attribute these flights and drops to my nerves, but that attribution doesn't mean the experiences have no meaning for me or haven't been important to who I am. What I think about the event affects the event itself. Epileptics also have auras—smells, sensations, and feelings of gloom, fear, or ecstasy that may precede a seizure. Throughout medical history, physicians have made links between illness and character. Researchers have speculated about migraine personalities in an effort to look for shared traits among the sufferers, but so many people have these headaches, along with various kinds of auras, that the hope of finding a migraine type has been mostly abandoned. With people who have temporal lobe epilepsy, however, there seem to be some broadly shared characteristics, including a tendency to be religious. Hippocrates first linked epilepsy to religiosity around 400 B.C., an observation that has been reiterated over time, into the modern era.[156] Emil Kraepelin, the famous turn-of-the-century doctor whose rigorous classifications of psychiatric disorders were highly influential, also noted that epileptics appeared to have strong spiritual leanings.[157]

The association of pathology with personality brings us yet again to a larger question: What are we? To what degree can beliefs, including religious ones, be linked to a person's neurobiology? Many people are comfortable with the idea that an illness like epilepsy, or a stroke or head injury, can alter a person's character but are perhaps less sanguine about the idea that each one of us discovers "truths" through his nervous system. Despite the fact that my parents displayed only conventional adherence to Lutheranism, I was not only pious as a child, I was quietly fervent. Later, when my belief in God fell away, I lost the piety but retained the fervency. What has remained in its stead is a deeply felt sense of meaning unaccompanied by dogma.

A number of popular articles in recent years have trumpeted the discovery of a "God spot" located in the temporal lobe of the brain. In 1997, the *Los Angeles Times* noted, " 'There may be dedicated neural machinery in the temporal lobe concerned with religion,' the team reported."[158] Notice the curious collapse of semantics into anatomy: *dedicated neural machinery in the temporal lobe concerned with religion*? The "team" is not saying that certain sensations and feelings experienced by human beings over the course of our history may have been attributed to the supernatural. They say religion is "hardwired" into our brains and, by doing so, they strongly resemble the nineteenth-century phrenologists who divided the brain into discrete, isolated regions, each of which had a specialized function. Tickle this spot and you'll believe in God. It is not hard to see this crude reduction of enormous historical and sociological realities to a bit of brain as philosophical naïveté at its worst. Another study disputed this finding, discovering "religion" all around the brain, including in those areas associated with emotional attachment, maternal care, and a child's early bonding with its mother. Surely, religious feeling is not a single entity. Rounding up religious epileptics or a group of Carmelite nuns, asking them to think about religion, and then testing their galvanic skin responses or putting them in fMRIs is bound to reap mixed results.

It does seem plain, however, that some people are more vulnerable to what Freud called "the oceanic feeling" than others. Freud declared that he did not have it but recognized its presence in other people. After a conversation with the novelist Romain Rolland, he wrote about the phenomenon in *Civilization and Its Discontents*:

> It is a feeling he [Rolland] would call a sensation of "eternity," a feeling as of something limitless, unbounded—as it were, "oceanic." This feeling, he adds, is a purely subjective fact, not an article of faith; it brings with it no assurance of personal immortality, but it is the source of the religious energy which is seized upon by the various Churches and religious systems, and doubtless also exhausted by them. One may, he thinks, call oneself religious on the ground of this oceanic feeling alone, even if one rejects every belief and every illusion.[159]

Freud speculates that this oceanic quality is an implicit memory of our early life when our egos were not fully separated from the world around us. His idea resonates with those of the researchers who found a connection between religious feeling and mother-child attachment. This forgotten period, according to Freud, then persists as a sensation of oneness with the world. Infancy is irretrievable. Its memories live underground. To what extent they return by stealth or are triggered by various catalysts remains an ongoing question, but what Freud understood through his conversation with Rolland was that "oceanic" does not necessarily mean a set of religious beliefs.

THE TASK OF DIAGNOSIS is to abstract "illness" from "person." Measles is one thing. It comes and goes. The spots move from one person to another. It is caused by a single pathogen. But when does illness become person? In 1975, Norman Geschwind and a fellow doctor, Stephen Waxman, published a paper about the shared characteristics they had noticed in their patients with temporal lobe epilepsy between seizures (called the *interictal* period): an increased religiosity or concern with ethical issues and a deepening of emotions, which vacillated with irritability. They also seemed to have a lowered sex drive and hypergraphia—many of them had a need to write, sometimes compulsively.[160]

By religiosity, Geschwind was referring to a feeling more related to Freud's oceanic feeling and Baruss's extraordinary transcendence than to formal theology. Religious and artistic figures as diverse as Saint Paul, Muhammad, Joan of Arc, Saint Teresa of Avila, Fyodor Dostoyevsky, Gustave Flaubert, Søren Kierkegaard, Vincent van Gogh, Guy de Maupassant, Marcel Proust, Lewis Carroll, and Alfred, Lord Tennyson have all been diagnosed either during or after their lifetimes with temporal lobe epilepsy.[161] Postmortem diagnoses of the very gifted and very famous have been appearing in book and paper form since the beginnings of modern medicine. It now seems clear that Flaubert had epilepsy, although he was also diagnosed with neurosis and hysteria; Dostoyevsky certainly had epilepsy (although Freud famously diagnosed him with hystero-epilepsy); Saint Paul's conversion on the road to Damascus appears to have been connected to a seizure; Saint Teresa has been diagnosed with epilepsy, hysteria, and migraine; van Gogh, epilepsy, lead poisoning, Ménière's disease, schizophrenia, bipolar disorder, and other illnesses. Lewis Carroll is claimed by neurologists as a temporal lobe epileptic and a migraineur. Symptoms can lead us down many roads, especially when you are diagnosing a patient who has been dead for years. Scrutinizing diaries, letters, texts, and artworks for neurological clues has its limitations.

As a girl, I drew constantly, an urge that later shifted to writing, and I often had a sense that there was an ineffable presence beyond me. My sex drive seems normal (whatever that means), but I have often felt I am too passionate in social situations and too intolerant of small talk, although I work hard to lower the intensity of my presence. I confessed to Dr. L. that I have sometimes wondered if I had it—a temporal lobe personality. But then again, my identifications are mobile. I empathize with lots of illnesses. Like countless first-year medical students, immersed in the symptoms of one disease after another, I am alert to the tingles and pangs, the throbs and quivers of my mortal body, each one of which is potentially a sign of *the end*.

No doubt because of my own peculiar visions and elations, mystics in all traditions fascinate me, and I have read about many of them. However one interprets these transcendent states, mystical experiences are genuine, take any number of forms, and can be spontaneous or induced by drugs, meditation, or even repetitive drumming or music. In his book *Major Trends in Jewish Mysticism,* Gershom Scholem quotes a disciple of Abraham Abulafia's who after two weeks of meditation began to shake: "Strong trembling seized me and I could summon no strength, my hair stood on end, and it was as if I were not of this world."[162] I was in high school doing research on Christian mystics when I first ran into earlier versions of "God spots," medical explanations for hearing voices, having visions, and euphoric feelings. Altered states of mind have long been viewed as pathological and, as such, they are explained away. In *Varieties of Religious Experience,* William James calls this method of elimination "medical materialism":

> Medical materialism finishes up Saint Paul by calling his vision on the road to Damascus a discharging lesion of the occipital cortex, he being an epileptic. It snuffs out Saint Teresa as an hysteric, Saint Francis of Assisi as an hereditary degenerate. . . . And medical materialism then thinks the spiritual authority of all such personages is successfully undermined.

James goes on to say that modern psychology accepts "psycho-physical connections" and the overall "dependence of mental states upon bodily conditions." It follows therefore that all states of mind are organic in this sense:

Scientific theories are organically conditioned just as much as religious emotions are; and if we knew the facts intimately enough, we should doubtless see the liver determining the dicta of the sturdy atheist as decisively as it does those of the Methodist under conviction anxious about his soul. When it alters in one way the blood that percolates it, we get the Methodist, when in another way, we get the atheist form of mind. So of all of our raptures and our drynesses, our longings and pantings, our questions and beliefs. They are equally organically founded, be they of religious or of non-religious content.[163]

James did not believe that this was the end of the matter, as the many pages that follow this passage demonstrate. Neither livers nor neurons, despite their importance, will suffice as explanations for spiritual or intellectual beliefs and experiences. The engineer who rejected empathy is no less subject to his bodily reality than Saint Paul. James's thought echoes Dostoyevsky's meditation on illness and feeling in *The Idiot*. "What if it is a disease?" his epileptic hero, Prince Myshkin, asks himself. "What does it matter that it is an abnormal tension, if the result, if the moment of sensation, remembered and analyzed in a state of health, turns out to be harmony and beauty brought to their highest point of perfection, and gives a feeling, undivined and undreamt of till then, of completeness, proportion, reconciliation, and an ecstatic and prayerful fusion in the highest synthesis of life?"[164] Although sometimes the morbid is also the transcendent, the transcendent cannot be reduced to the morbid.

Dostoyevsky exploited his epileptic auras in his novels, and they undoubtedly influenced his religious beliefs. Flaubert never explicitly used his seizures in his fiction. Emma Bovary's romantic effusions are wholly different from Prince Myshkin's elation, not the least because Flaubert kept an ironic if sympathetic distance from his theatrical heroine. Dostoyevsky and Flaubert may have had the same disease, but their personalities and their art developed along entirely different paths.

BROADLY DEFINED AS DISEASED OR OTHERWISE, mystical experiences seem to dissolve the boundaries of the self. If stories from the neurology ward make anything clear, it is that the borders of the self we imagine are mutable. Migraine auras have sometimes borne me into a sense of happy immersion in the world, but the shaking woman cuts me in two. The former creates a sense of wholeness and harmony, the latter, disruption and division. When the shaking happens, my narrating first-person subject seems to go in one direction and my recalcitrant body in another, which illustrates the fact that I locate myself through that inner voice. Language is intimate to my sense of self—that endlessly ruminating verbal interior that accompanies me as I go through my daily activities. I feel I own that commentary, that I form it to match what I am thinking or feeling or seeing, and when I speak aloud, I express myself with greater care to be understood, just as I listen intently when I want to comprehend what another person is saying. But sometimes words become unhinged from self-feeling and float off into foreign territory and are heard as if they are coming from invisible others. People hear voices.

In his *Confessions,* Saint Augustine writes about his profound spiritual crisis, during which he hears a child's voice saying over and over, *"Tolle, lege"* (Pick up and read).[165] Joan of Arc heard voices, acted on them, and found herself in the French court and on the battlefield. William Blake both saw and heard angels. The list is long and includes Muhammad, the Sufi poet Rumi, Yeats, and Rilke, all of whom listened to voices during periods of high tension and emotion. In one of my hospital classes, I taught a woman student who spoke to God regularly, and he answered her. She had a direct line to the divinity because he was, she told me, her *husband.* Of course, not all hallucinated voices have a revelatory religious quality. A friend of mine related the story of a man he knew who was tormented by nasty voices whenever he turned on the water to take a bath: "You dirty, shitty, little scumbag!" The history of hearing voices is as old as the history of convulsive illness. Socrates heard voices, and in *The Iliad* and *The Odyssey,* the voices of the gods guide the heroes. Whatever the content of the words uttered, intrusive voices are always experienced as not coming from the self, which makes them qualitatively different from our inner speech or internal narrators, although some researchers have theorized that inner speech is somehow deflected in these experiences. Like the alien hands of split-brain patients, the paralyzed limbs of neglect patients, Neil's remembering writing hand, and the automatic texts that flowed from the pens of innumerable poets, they are *not* understood as something that *belongs* to *me*.

In his book *The Origin of Consciousness in the Breakdown of the Bicameral Mind* (1976), Julian Jaynes argued that before the end of the second millennium B.C. human beings had a bicameral mind, rather than a unitary consciousness—the two hemispheres of the brain functioned separately—and when under duress, these earlier people heard voices, often commands, that originated in the right hemisphere and were interpreted as coming from higher powers. It all changed when an oral tradition became a literate one, a reading and writing culture. According to the bicameral theory, our brains were altered by the advent of literacy.[166] Jaynes has his admirers and his detractors, and his big idea remains highly controversial, but there are those who have reexamined it lately, and some studies have suggested that there is increased right hemisphere activity in people when they are having auditory hallucinations.[167] There is no consensus, however, about what is actually going on in the brains of those who hear voices.

It is now known though that while language function is still considered to be dominated by the left hemisphere, our right hemisphere is not speechless, and it plays an important role in certain aspects of language, such as understanding the emotional content of a sentence. Early human experiences with language—a parent lovingly repeating a child's name, the incantations of nursery rhymes, the lyrics of lullabies, and the musical sounds of a mother's comforting voice—appear to be part of right-hemispheric, not left, cognition.[168] Early parental negative commands like *No* or *Stop* would also fall into this category, as do powerful taboo words, the censored expletives. The nineteenth-century neurologist John Hughlings Jackson theorized about the difference in language function between the hemispheres. By carefully observing his patients, as well as studying the work of other doctors (Paul Broca, in particular), he determined that the right hemisphere was responsible for automatic expressions, the explosive unwilled ejaculations of words that cannot be repeated willfully. The rapid-fire verbal outpourings of Tourette's syndrome appear to demonstrate this very well. When the right and left hemispheres function together, Jackson maintained, the automatic merges with the *voluntary* use of words and becomes ordinary speech.[169] I would underline the fact that what Jackson's merger means is that when the hemispheres meet, *speech gains an owner*—the first-person subject. It is also interesting that since the early sixties neurologists have noticed that illiterate people who sustain damage to the language areas of the left brain do not suffer from the same aphasic problems that literate people do,[170] an observation that doesn't prove but also doesn't weaken Jaynes's sweeping historical idea. Learning to read and write do appear to strengthen left-brain dominance.

There is also a hypothesis that people in hypomanic and manic states may temporarily become bilateral for language, using both hemispheres more equally. An unusually high number of poets have suffered from bipolar disorder, with its dramatic highs and lows, and some scholars have argued that poetry, more than literary prose or ordinary communicative speech, draws on the language strengths of the right brain, which may help explain some of the stories about automatic writing, abrupt inspirations, and the feeling that a work is not willed but dictated. The many poets and writers who probably had what is now called bipolar disorder include Paul Celan, Anne Sexton, Robert Lowell, Theodore Roethke, John Berryman, James Schuyler, and Virginia Woolf. My own sense of the writing of manic patients—or, indeed, any psychotic patient—is that both their prose and their poetry are far more vivid, musical, witty, and original than that of so-called normal people. Religious and cosmological themes are very common, even though their writing often lacks both logic and narrative sequence. A significant number of my creative-writing patients have also heard voices, and several of them were strikingly hypergraphic. P., an intelligent, articulate, highly educated woman in one of my classes, a manic-depressive, told me that she had written a seven-thousand-page manuscript in a matter of a few months during one of her sustained, joyous flights.

Hearing voices is probably most strongly associated with schizophrenia. Some schizophrenics are plagued by regular onslaughts of voices—sometimes malignant, sometimes not—whose endless commentary, scolding, or directives interfere with the everyday business of waking, working, eating, and family life. Nevertheless, since Jaynes published his book in 1976, a number of studies have shown that auditory hallucinations are quite common in people who have not been diagnosed with a mental illness. Daniel Smith, the author of *Muses, Madmen and Prophets: Rethinking the History, Science, and Meaning of Auditory Hallucinations,* became interested in the subject because his father and grandfather both heard voices a lot of the time. Neither man was schizophrenic or manic-depressive. I found it touching that Smith worked hard to induce voices in himself. He even immersed himself in a sensory deprivation tank, hoping to have the experience, but to no avail.[171]

How the voices are interpreted varies from person to person. Some people, especially schizophrenics, explain the nattering inside or outside their heads as invasive visitors from outer space, angels, implanted radios, or, more recently, computer chips, while other voice hearers seem to know that the voices are produced internally. Schizophrenics are more likely to confabulate an answer, to be delusional. After all, a hallucination is simply an experience that is not part of inter-subjective reality. If I hear bells ringing, ask you whether you hear them too, and all that meets your ears is the white noise of my living room, you have reason to believe something odd is going on with me.

AFTER THE TREE-PLANTING CEREMONY in honor of my father, my mother, my three sisters, and I fell into conversation in Liv's kitchen. We discussed my mysterious convulsion for a while, and then, summoning another neurological conundrum, I mentioned my own auditory hallucinations. I heard voices at around the ages of eleven and twelve, not all the time, but once in a while. They arrived when I was alone and spoke in a mechanical chorus, repeating phrases over and over, which made me feel that they wanted to push me into their insistent, threatening rhythm, to take me over. Liv said that she had heard punitive voices around the same age and that she'd battled them with her own words, trying to drown them out. My sister Ingrid then announced that when she was six or seven she had heard a voice, which she'd believed was her conscience speaking aloud to her. One night, dismayed by the chatterer in her head, she had gone up to our parents and asked them what she should do about "Jiminy Cricket." Pinocchio was my sister's sole reference for the phenomenon, one that made perfect sense, but understandably, our parents had no idea what she was talking about. It turned out that my mother had never heard voices, nor had my sister Asti. Asti confessed to feeling a little left out—the only nonhallucinating sister among the four of us. Later, my daughter, Sophie, now twenty-one, told me that she too had heard voices when she was younger. My father once said to me after my grandfather died, "I sometimes hear Father calling me." He announced this very simply as a fact and with obvious feeling, but I had no sense that he regarded it as troublesome. He loved his father and sometimes he heard him. Perhaps that voice was the return of an old auditory memory coming from the right hemisphere of his brain— the sound of his father calling him home. At various junctures in my life, I have hallucinated both my parents saying my name. The phenomenon seems to run in the family. My father, three out of four of us sisters, and my daughter all hear or heard voices.

Another small story illustrates the emotional, brief, and adamant character of at least one form of hearing a voice, which must emanate from somewhere in the self but is clearly heard as coming from another person. During the siege in Sarajevo, my husband and I had a houseguest from that city, a theater director, who had staged one of my husband's books as a play. Over the course of the few days he spent with us, he told us stories about friendships betrayed, unspeakable acts of cruelty, and the ongoing deprivations of the war. Late one morning, he left our house in Brooklyn for a meeting in Manhattan. I said good-bye to him and returned to work at my desk. A few minutes after I had sat down, I heard him call out, "Help me!" I rushed down two flights of stairs to the door, expecting to see him splayed on the front steps. But there was no sign of him. It had been a hallucination. I had never heard this friend say, "Help me." The voice, *his voice,* was not an acoustic memory of a phrase he had uttered, but, I would suggest, as in dreams, it was a condensation of days of remembered dialogue into a single vivid cry for help, unleashed suddenly and involuntarily from a deep, emotional place in my mind.

Since that strange but memorable call for help, the only times I hear voices regularly anymore are at night. As I lie in bed on the threshold between wakefulness and sleep, I often hear both male and female voices utter short emphatic sentences and, every once in a while, my name. Sometimes I tell myself to remember what they have said, but I rarely do. They are the audible ephemera of the time when full consciousness recedes and my mind seems to jump onto two wholly separate tracks: the heard and the seen. Invisible strangers talk in short bursts while I watch the fabulous, often brilliantly colored hypnogogic hallucinations, both figurative and abstract, that pass before my closed eyelids. These are phenomena at the limen of sleep and dreams. Like dreams, they do not feel willed. Unlike dreams, I listen to the voices but never speak back to them, and I watch the visions as an observer, not as a first-person actor. Once, I saw myself in those presleep pictures. At first, I didn't recognize whom I was looking at, but then I realized that it was an image of my younger self. I was holding my daughter when she was still a baby. Sophie had lain her head on my shoulder, and then, like everything else on that metamorphosing screen, we vanished.

If there is any lesson to be taken from this short tour of transcendent feelings and alien voices, it is how hard it can be to classify the phenomena. Sometimes such experiences are linked to an illness such as epilepsy or to a psychosis; sometimes they aren't. If they become unbearable to you or to others close to you, you may end up in a hospital for treatment. Otherwise, elevated, even rapturous moods and intermittent voices may simply become integrated into your daily life or find their way into your poetry. They may, in fact, make life feel more rather than less meaningful, and you will inevitably read them from the perspective of your own narrative history. Rumi's and Rilke's ecstatic illuminations may share common traits and a physiological ground, but each man's transports were contextualized in a different way because each man lived inside his own language and culture. What is certain is that it becomes difficult to separate *personality* from these lived experiences, however curious, especially if they recur, and how one makes sense of them is crucial to living with them.

I RECEIVE A THREE-PAGE single-spaced letter from Dr. L., a description of our meeting and the process ahead. This woman is thorough. A sentence catches my attention: "In summary the history and physical exam indicate that she has classical migraine, occasionally morphing into status migrainosis, and is concerned that she may have temporal lobe epilepsy based on the history and the characteristics of the episodes." Alas, my life is lived in the borderland of Headache. Most days I wake up with migraine, which subsides after coffee, but nearly every day includes some pain, some clouds in the head, heightened sensitivities to light, sounds, moisture in the air. Most afternoons I lie down to do my biofeedback exercises, which calm my nervous system. The headache is me, and understanding this has been my salvation. Perhaps the trick will now be to integrate the shaking woman as well, to acknowledge that she, too, is part of myself.

I SIT DOWN in the small waiting room of the MRI office with a standard form. The insurance company has approved only the brain MRI, not the one for my cervical spine. When I write down my name and address, I realize I am about to make an error. Under "City," I almost write Northfield, the town where I grew up, not Brooklyn. I am flabbergasted. I have lived in Brooklyn for twenty-seven years and New York City for thirty. What is going on? Without being conscious of it, I must have traveled to a time in a house I cannot remember. All I have retained of those early days is my first address: 910 West Second Street, Northfield, Minnesota. The interior of that house is purely imaginary, and its occupants are characters I have shaped through the stories told to me by other people. My young mother stands over a feverish baby whose body twitches and jerks. I now live on another Second Street, one in Brooklyn, New York. The gaffe was formed in a mental underground where one town replaced another, two streets became one, and past and present mingled in a single paroxysmal image. What pokes up into daylight is one word: *Northfield*. As my hand moved the pen across the paper and filled in the information, the habitual act, performed thousands of times since I learned to write, was relocated, as if I were still a girl at my school desk filling in my name and address for the teacher.

WHEN THEY TAPE MY head and slide me into the long tube, I feel anxious. The technician explains that it will take about a half an hour. He gives me a ball to squeeze if I discover I "don't like it in there"—in other words, if I panic. I don't like it in there, but I don't panic. I tell myself to do biofeedback and open myself up to the experience as any good phenomenologist would. Although I am wearing earplugs, the machine's noise is deafening. I feel I have been immobilized at an extraterrestrial rock concert, the rhythms of which arrive as incessant whacks to my head. I try counting the beats. Three long blasts of sound, then six shorter taps. I can assimilate this pattern, but after that a speed hammer arrives. The concert has turned into a robot on amphetamines using me as his drum. I find it hard to remain still. The sounds slam into my head, but I also feel them in my torso, my arms, and my legs. My face convulses involuntarily, and I emerge dazed after my half hour of encapsulation.

As I leave the building, I am aware of the haze lowering in my head. My vision has changed. Outside, the sunlight hurts. The dizziness arrives, and the nausea. Then sharp pain and the stupefying exhaustion that slows my every step. The MRI has triggered a migraine. The test to search for scars in my brain that would support a diagnosis of epilepsy has knocked that poor organ into familiar territory—the land of Headache. The irony makes me smile. I don't fight migraine anymore. I embrace it, and by doing that, I am also, strangely, able to feel less pain.

In *Gravity and Grace,* Simone Weil writes:

> Headaches. At a certain moment, the pain is lessened by projecting it into the universe, but the universe is impaired; the pain is more intense when it comes home again, but something in me does not suffer and remains in contact with a universe which is not impaired.[172]

Weil, philosopher, mystic, and political activist, struggled with crippling headaches. She was a chronic migraineur whose personality traits strongly resemble those Norman Geschwind linked to temporal lobe epilepsy. She would have to be described as hyposexual; she never had a lover, but she wrote with unflagging energy and was deeply religious. If she had seizures, they were not diagnosed. Geschwind did not believe that his list of traits was limited to epileptics, a fact that both broadens the syndrome and weakens it as a diagnostic tool. Weil was a person of rare intellectual gifts whose experiences led her far from materialism into the realm of extraordinary transcendence. (I suspect she could have unscrambled any image Professor Baruss put before her.) Weil's life is yet another example of how the neurological and the psychological overlap to shape beliefs, both of a spiritual and a nonspiritual nature, as James argued. Isolating Weil's migraines from her personality and her ideas can only create false categories, which is not to say that she was *made* by her headaches. She, like every one of us, was a being who accumulated a self over time. A genetic tendency toward migraine and the ongoing experience of the headaches, as well as the neurological instability that comes with them, were essential pieces in the story of her life, as were Dostoyevsky's seizures. Epilepsy and migraine do not, of course, belong exclusively to the gifted among us. One person's hypergraphic outpourings may be brilliant and another's mere drivel. Illness does not necessarily produce insight.

But Weil's passage about headache is typically perspicacious. She dissolves the border between outside and inside. Her injury is internal and external, her pain fierce, and yet some portion of her suspends it and grips what is not hurt but whole. I know from experience that it is possible to work even with severe headaches, to feel pain but to learn not to pay attention to it in a way that will only exacerbate the misery. Focus and worry make headaches worse. Distraction and meditation make them better.

In *Pain: The Science of Suffering,* the neuroscientist Patrick Wall argues that pain is not measurable by the usual methods of science. In study after study, he writes, researchers have gathered a group of "subjects," administered a painful stimulus to each one, and then monitored and compared their volunteers' physiological responses. This is how science proceeds, but Wall maintains that the artificial context of these experiments distorts the realities of pain. The subjects know the scientists aren't going to cast them into a state of prolonged agony, and if they hurt too much, they can yell, Stop! Wall refers to this laboratory environment as *pain without suffering:* "the measurement of pain in these circumstances has been carried out in thousands of trials. Inherent in these trials is the concept of a pure sensation of pain liberated from perceptions and meanings. Many believe such a sensation exists. I do not."[173] Wall points out that despite experiments conducted in exactly the same way with identical verbal instructions, the upper threshold of tolerable pain changes from culture to culture. Results also depend on who is giving the instructions—a man or a woman, a professor, a technician, or a student.

None of these findings startles me. If one knows pain will end (this is a twenty-four-hour stomach flu and I will soon be better), it is more bearable than a mild ache you have been told is killing you. My roots are in Scandinavia, where stoicism is highly valued. Swimming in ice water is viewed as admirable, but in another culture it might be regarded as foolish or downright insane, and a given person's response to that dip in the frigid deep will not just *appear to be* different, according to its meaning for him, it will *be* different, and not just psychologically but neurobiologically. You can't parse the two. Most people are more impressed by professors than by students and will be more inclined to parade their toughness when face-to-face with *Herr Doktor* himself, as opposed to an underling reading from a script. I suspect man-on-man encounters often involve testosterone-fueled competition, something women are less likely to engage in. And pain is always emotional. Fear and depression keep constant company with chronic hurting. *It will never go away; I will always be in pain; I feel so sad* are the mantras of those who wake, slog through the day, and retire every night with everlasting pain of one kind or another. When I had my two bouts of status migrainosis, each one of which lasted about a year, I continually checked my pain: *Was it lighter? A bit.* Hope waved a victorious flag inside me. *Soon it will disappear and go away forever! Was it worse? Yes, it was definitely worse.* I lowered the flag and returned to battle. Hour after hour, day after day, month after month, I tracked the ups and downs of my wretched head. After I had seen Dr. E. and learned to meditate with his machine (there is essentially no difference between biofeedback and various forms of Eastern meditation), I retired from the headache vigilance squad. I stopped paying so much attention to my pain. It is there often, and every once in a while it becomes violent and I must stop working and lie down, but I neither despair nor believe it will vanish forever. My pain is qualitatively different from what it was when I was younger. I suffer less because my perception of the pain I feel and the meaning I attach to it have changed.

Patrick Wall died of cancer in 2001. In his book, published the previous year, he does not widen his thoughts to include scientific research on other aspects of human life, but he could easily have done so. Essentially, Wall is saying: pain cannot be separated from our perception of pain, and those perceptions have meanings. Such perceptions involve an individual's nervous system inside a particular body in relation to a particular environment—to culture, language, and other people (present and absent). Pain happens within the lived body of a subject, not inside the hypothetical, objective, inert body of *Gray's Anatomy*. Is there a "pure sensation" of anything that can be attributed to neural networks rather than to a sentient, thinking, embodied human being living in a world? And that problem doesn't even touch on the befuddling dilemma of the word itself, *pain,* used here by the researchers to mean what happens after a "subject" gets an electric shock, a pinprick, or a slap. How do I know what pain means except for what it means to me? For years, I have been puzzling over Wittgenstein's meditations on language and pain in his *Philosophical Investigations:* "[Pain] is not a *something,*" he announces, "but not a *nothing* either! The conclusion was only that a nothing would serve just as well as a something about which nothing could be said." The philosopher goes on to recommend "a radical break with the idea that language always functions in one way, always serves the same purpose: to convey thoughts—which may be about houses, pains, good and evil, or anything else you please."[174] The slippery character of language is in its use, which changes from speaker to speaker. Scientists forget this with stunning regularity.

I have always found it comic when a doctor asks me to rate my pain on a scale of 1 to 10. Here numbers take the place of words. Rate my pain in relation to what? The worst pain I've ever had? Do I remember the worst pain? I can't retrieve it as pain, only as an articulated memory or an empathetic relation to my past self: childbirth hurt, migraines hurt, the pain in my cracked elbow hurt. Which one was a 6, a 7? Is your 4 my 5? Is Charlie's 9 Daya's 2? Does a 10 actually exist, or is it a sort of ideal representation of the unbearable? Do you expire after a 10? The notion that degrees of pain can be charted by numbers is ludicrous but routine. The attempt to avoid ambiguity only increases it.

The change in my own pain is psychobiological. My thoughts have been crucial to reducing my pain. As the authors of the paper on placebo effects I cited earlier acknowledged, "cognitive factors" affect neurochemistry. What we have always thought of as mental can influence what we have always thought of as physical. No one can explain how these complex mechanisms work, but activity in the prefrontal, executive portion of the brain does appear to regulate and inhibit many cerebral functions. People with obsessive-compulsive disorder can reduce their intense needs to wash, check, count, or touch with simple cognitive behavioral techniques—resisting the impulse over greater and greater periods of time. The talking cure has been shown to be as effective as drugs for people with mild or moderate depression, although often both are used as treatment.[175]

Human beings are repetitive animals. All meaning is generated through repetition. When I come upon a word I don't know, I have to look it up and hope that the next time around I will remember what *pruriginous* means. As soon as it is repeated, the novel ceases to be novel. Shaking once is different from shaking twice. In psychiatric and neurological illnesses, repetition often appears to be compulsive, an unstoppable urge to return to the same thing, something Freud noticed in his own patients and wrote about. In the hospital when I am teaching, it is evident that many patients in my classes have fallen into neuropsychological ruts—the inability to lift themselves out of a pattern of relentless morbid repetition. Depressed people generate one gloomy thought after another, for example, but there are times when, if urged to refocus their energies in a writing assignment, they find themselves, at least for the moment, jogged out of their trenches of misery. "I remember my mother's chicken gravy and how good it was."

THE STORY OF THE SHAKING WOMAN is the narrative of a repeated event that, over time, gained multiple meanings when seen from various perspectives. What first appeared as an anomaly became frightening and emotionally charged after its recurrence. Can we say that my responses over time were psychological rather than neurological? Where do we draw the line? Scientists routinely talk about *levels*—the neural level and the psychological level. They use a spatial metaphor. At the bottom are neurons. A step up is the psyche. We climb a ladder, not unlike the medieval chain of being. The visible exists on the first rung, and the invisible, psychic stuff on the second. A neuron can be seen. Your thoughts cannot. Are neurons more real than thoughts? Scientists often talk about neural representations. How do neurons *represent* things? A representation is an image or symbol for something else. How does that work? Is there a stratum *brain* and on top of it *mind,* and these two are somehow interconnected? Other scientists and philosophers add a third tier for our global, social, and cultural life—what's outside us. Isn't it possible that this visual metaphor is problematic, that the very idea of hierarchical *levels* is flawed? Can brain, psyche, and culture really be distinguished so neatly? Aren't we born into a world of meaningful others and things? I do not have an answer to these questions but, like Wall, I ask whether it is possible to isolate an experience such as pain from its context.

On the other hand, I do not think biology should be ignored. My attraction to Merleau-Ponty's thought is that he, like James, emphasizes the corporeal reality of human existence: "Visible and mobile, my body is a thing among things; it is caught in the fabric of the world, and its cohesion is that of a thing. But because it moves itself and sees, it holds things in a circle around itself."[176] The recent fashion for social construction—the study of how ideas are formed in a culture and shape our thought—has spawned innumerable books with titles such as *The Social Construction of X* and *The*

Invention of Y. Often these books have a political agenda. By revealing how the idea of womanhood, for example, has been "constructed" and "reconstructed" over time, it may be possible to lift the onus of sexism by showing that femininity is not a static entity but a fluctuating idea subject to the influence of history and society. It would be very hard to argue against this, but sometimes the intense focus on the social turns human beings into floating busts. Although there are hermaphrodites, most of us are born either male or female and there are biological differences between the two sexes, which does not necessarily imply the need to oppress one or the other. When I gave birth to my daughter, I felt my body had taken over the proceedings. Pregnancy and giving birth are, of course, socially constructed. Mary Douglas points out in *Purity and Danger* that in Lele culture an unborn child is perceived as dangerous to other people in the community, and a pregnant woman must take care not to approach sick people for fear of making them worse.[177] Sophie was born in 1987 and, at least in my circles, it was considered a badge of honor to deliver "naturally," without drugs. Now the epidural is routine. Pain is out. Pain relief is in. "Constructions" vary from culture to culture and change within cultures. But from another perspective, birth is a physical event that is always fundamentally the same. Sex and birth are both culturally generated ideas and facts of nature.

In his book *The Social Construction of What?* Ian Hacking discusses psychiatric illness and proposes that there is room for both construction and biology. He points out that classifications affect people. They interact with them, are what Hacking calls *interactive kinds*. Being labeled a schizophrenic will affect you, and you may find yourself in the subculture of psychiatry because of it, a land unto itself with white-coated physicians, pharmacological interventions, locked wards, dance therapy, and even writing classes that will influence how you think about yourself. This does not mean that there is no inherent biology at work, which goes on entirely unaffected by what is thought about it; a genetic predisposition to schizophrenia would qualify as an *indifferent kind,* Hacking's version of the philosophical term *natural kind.*[178] Sometimes, however, as Hacking well knows, how you think does affect your biology. When I do biofeedback I am altering my nervous system. All of this means that hard science is vital. Observing a single cell can reap extraordinary results. Studying the lowest life-forms can tell us something about ourselves. The important position science has come to occupy in the culture is not accidental. As Jürgen Habermas has argued, science has gained its ascendancy in the modern world because it has demonstrated great power over the natural world.[179] One need only think of the atom bomb or, on a brighter note, antibiotics.

The language we use is crucial to our understanding, however, and many of the intellectual models used to explain *how it is* with us human beings are limited, inadequate, or downright obtuse. Categories, borders, distinctions, and metaphors such as ladders, roots, theaters, computers, blueprints, machinery, or locked rooms are both necessary and useful, but they have to be recognized for what they are: convenient images to aid comprehension—which necessarily leave out or misconstrue or distort an ambiguous, shifting reality. It is human to want to pin things down and give them a name. No one really wants to live like Borges's hero, a person so attentive to the shifting plethora of the phenomenal world that the dog seen at three-fourteen deserves a name different from the one seen at three-fifteen. And yet, the story reminds us that all abstraction comes at a cost. Doctors need diagnoses, names for groups of symptoms, and so do patients. At last, I have a sign to hang on my disparate aches and pains or shakes and wobbles. Or do I?

THE MRI COMES UP WITH NOTHING. My brain looks normal, no swellings or tumors or thinning. I will have to battle with the insurance company to get the second one, on my spine. Of course, a significant percentage of people who have seizures also have normal neuroimaging results. In the *Journal of Neurology, Neurosurgery, and Psychiatry,* I find a paper titled "Is It Worth Pursuing Surgery for Epilepsy in Patients with Normal Neuroimagining?"[180] The authors believe it is, but, of course, they want to scoop out bits of brain that belong to people who are tortured by seizures though their doctors cannot find evidence of a lesion on the MRI results. Am I back at the beginning yet again? I now have a psychoanalyst-psychiatrist and a neurologist treating me, but neither of them can tell me who the shaking woman is.

WHILE HELPFUL, cutting the inside of a person (the neurological and the psychological) off from what is outside him (other people, language, the world) is artificial. The differences revealed by these incisions are a matter of focus, how to see and interpret an illness or symptom. Even if my tremor were hysterical, a form of dissociation, a personal metaphor for the unspeakable or for mourning or for an emotional conflict with my father that I have repressed, which then appeared as a psychogenic seizure, I doubt it would have taken that particular form if I didn't have a neurological predisposition to it, perhaps because of my feverish tremors as an infant, my seizure as a young woman in Paris before the long migraine, perhaps for some as-yet-not-identified reason. Many people—actors, musicians, surgeons, trial lawyers—are subject to a hand tremor before or at the onset of a performance, and many of them calm the quivering with a drug. My fits may simply be an extreme version of that more prosaic physical manifestation of anxiety. On the other hand, let us say that hidden somewhere in my brain, undetected by the MRI, or somewhere in my unexplored cervical spine area, there is a *lesion* that could be designated as the *cause* for shaking. I still don't believe I would have started shuddering if I had not been speaking about my father or standing on that old ground of memory or if I hadn't been facing family friends I had known since childhood. I would not have shaken that day if there had not been some strong, if hidden emotional catalyst. Genuine epileptic seizures are often triggered by powerful emotion. And what about the shudder in the Pyrenees? I climbed too fast in the thin air and lost my breath, which sent my already vulnerable system into convulsive motion. Hyperventilation can bring on seizures. Every person has a seizure threshold. Mine might be lower than average. Of course, I may be wrong about all of this.

Whatever the truth may be, the ups and downs of my own nervous system and my encounters with doctors illustrate the ambiguities of illness and diagnosis. The philosophical ideas that lie beneath calling one thing by one name and another by another often remain unexamined, and they may be determined more by intellectual fashions than by rigorous thought. The *New York Times* headline "Is Hysteria Real?" upholds the conventional belief: if you can see it, it's real and physical. If you can't, it's unreal and mental. Or, rather, most scientists agree that what's mental is really physical but can't describe how that works. Then again, for other scientists, there is no physical reality that can be understood as if we could leap out of our own heads and become objective; everything we live is given to us via the mental. The world is mind. Whatever the case may be, on a more pedestrian "level," there is no simple identifiable cause and effect to illuminate what exactly is wrong with me, no linear motion from one thing to another, but a number of factors that may or may not play a role in the vagaries of the shaking woman's path.

A FRIEND OF MINE has a sister who has had epileptic seizures since she was a little girl. L. used to wake up at night to see her sister flailing and flapping in the bed next to her own. L. told me that her sister does not feel alienated from her auras and fits. In fact, they are so deeply part of her, she is reluctant to medicate them away. In his essay "Witty Ticky Ray," Oliver Sacks describes a Tourette's patient who, after his tics vanished with a drug, missed them so much that he began taking weekend holidays from his pharmaceuticals, so he could tic again with happy abandon.[181] The bipolar patient P. who produced the seven-thousand-page manuscript made it clear to me that she mourned her mania terribly. I felt sure that once the authorities released her from the hospital, she would stop taking her lithium. After his voices stopped, a schizophrenic patient felt alone for the first time in years and wasn't sure he liked it. In her book *The Midnight Disease*, the neurologist Alice Flaherty describes and analyzes her postpartum hypergraphia, which began not long after she gave birth to twin boys who died. She was also visited by a host of metaphorical images that made the world around her feel uncommonly vivid but were intrusive and distracting. When a drug brought them to a halt, she writes, "the world became so dead that my psychiatrist and I lowered the doses until I could have at least some of my tyrannical metaphors back."[182] What if it is a disease? Prince Myshkin asked. I, too, have become curiously attached to my migraines and the various feelings that have accompanied them. I cannot really see where the illness ends and I begin; or, rather, the headaches are me, and rejecting them would mean expelling myself from myself.

None of us chooses chronic illness. It chooses us. Over time, L.'s sister did not accommodate her life to *having* tonic-clonic seizures; her seizures became woven into the very fabric of her conscious identity, her narrative self, as are my migraines, P.'s mania, and Dr. Flaherty's metaphors and hypergraphia, for better and for worse. Perhaps because she was a late arrival, I have had a much harder time integrating the shaking woman into my story, but as she becomes familiar, she is moving out of the third person and into the first, no longer a detested double but an admittedly handicapped part of my self.

Exactly what a self is remains controversial. The neuroscientist Jaak Panksepp maintains that human beings have a core self that can be located in the brain, a mammalian self outside of language but crucial to a state of wakeful awareness; the periaqueductal gray (PAG) region of the brain is a very small spot indeed, but when it is damaged, wakeful consciousness goes with it.[183] Antonio Damasio also proposes a core self, although he differs somewhat with Panksepp as to precisely where it is.[184] Both would agree that this core being is not the autobiographical self, not the person saying or writing "I remember."

Michael Gazzaniga, the scientist who worked with split-brain patients and coined the neat term "left-brain interpreter," marshals evidence for a view of the self through selection theory: "all we do in life is discover what was built into our brains."[185] According to Gazzaniga, the environmental influences on a person *select* from options that are already there. This apparently innocuous idea of innate ability—people do not fly, except in their dreams and on airplanes, because we have no native capacity for it—becomes chillier as the theory is extended into the social realm. It leads serially to other beliefs: that parents have very little influence on children (they are immune to instruction) and that social programs designed to support people with various problems are counterproductive because what individuals really need is to be thrown into survival mode. Cancer patients should be encouraged to "fight" their illnesses because the combat will help them live longer. Gazzaniga is one of several scientists who, when he publishes a book for a broad audience, has taken to throwing swords at the "blank slate" view of human beings.

Steven Pinker, a respected cognitive psychologist, has written several popular books about his field. He, too, rails against blank slaters.[186] The blank slate idea, often attributed to John Locke, argues that human beings are born blanks and then are written on by experience. But Locke did not disavow native human capacities. He was arguing against Descartes's theory of innate ideas, that there are universal truths we are all born with, shared by all people. Whatever his philosophical flaws may be, in *An Essay Concerning Human Understanding*, Locke delineates a developmental, interactive view of life: you need to have had the experience of red before you know what red is. In truth, it would be very difficult to find any serious proponent of a radical blank slate theory, just as one could not find a sane advocate of absolute biological determinism. Even the most extreme constructionist doesn't argue against genes. Even people who maintain that the self—or, rather, the "subject"—is a fiction founded in language, a figment that is constantly being recast in terms of the dominant ideology of a particular historical epoch, don't believe that human beings have no inherent capacity for speech. To put it bluntly: what is at issue here is emphasis—genes over experience or experience over genes.

Gazzaniga, Pinker, and many others believe, with good reason, that inside academic institutions, some scholars have stressed human malleability to a degree that is unfounded. But their confidence that research has proven, for example, that parents have no effect on their offspring is remarkable. I would direct them to the growing laboratory research on mammals that indicates that genetic makeup is modified by environmental factors, including maternal care.[187] Ideas quickly become beliefs, and beliefs quickly become bullets in ideological wars. What we are and how we're *made* is surely a battleground in one of those wars. The tough and the tender are constantly shooting off artillery at each other. Near the end of a PowerPoint presentation and lecture on the brain I attended in February 2009, the Harvard neuroscientist Hans Breiter turned to the image on his screen: a huge blue rectangle. Inside that rectangle was a tiny red square. "That's how much we know about the brain," he said, referring not to the vast blue but to the minute red spot. What we know often becomes an excuse to extrapolate endlessly, but my hunch is that most of the time intellectual humility takes one further than arrogance.

In Buddhism, the self is an illusion. There is no self. Some cognitive scientists agree with that formulation. Others don't. Freud's model of the self was dynamic, complex, divided into three, and provisional. He truly believed that science would elaborate on his ideas, and it has, albeit in many conflicting directions. In psychoanalytic object relations theory as it developed, the self is also plural. The images of important others inhabit us forever. D. W. Winnicott let more air into the psychic room than did Freud, whose model of mental structures is more confined, more likely to deal with fantasies and identifications than with real other people and actual experiences. Winnicott believed that we all have a true self, as well as false selves. Our social selves necessarily have false aspects—the polite smile or the "I'm fine" response to "How are you?"[188] I don't know what a self is. Defining it, whatever it is, is clearly a semantic problem, a question of borders and perception, as well as any psychobiological truths we might be able to discover.

I feel I have one—a self—but why? Is it everything that lies within the borders of my body? Not really. When I shook, it didn't feel like *me*. That was the problem. When did it arrive, that selfness? I don't remember, but I know that secrecy is part of it. There was a time when I believed my mother could look into my eyes and see guilt. In *What Maisie Knew*, Henry James identifies a new sense that has begun to stir in his child heroine:

> The stiff dolls on the dusky shelves began to move their arms and legs; old forms and phrases began to have a sense that frightened her. She had a new feeling, the feeling of danger; on which a new remedy rose to meet it, the idea of an inner self or, in other words, of concealment.[189]

Maisie discovers the place in us we retreat to, the place where we hide without being seen by others, the refuge we seek when we are afraid, and the dark sanctum that makes lies possible, but also daydreams and reveries and bad thoughts and intense internal dialogues. This is not the core biological self. It comes about at some half-remembered time in childhood. Other animals don't have it; it requires an understanding of a dual reality, that the verbal or emotional content of an inside self doesn't have to show itself to the outside. In other words, you have to be aware of what you are hiding to hide it. Very small children often narrate their thoughts aloud. At three, my daughter chattered away as she played: "The little piggy's going to bed all alone. Whoops, he falls off the bed! Better get back up. Don't cry, little piggy." But later, the narration stopped. Sophie could play for hours in silence, absorbed but not talking. Her narrator had gone inside. Is this when a turn is made? Is this inner arena of thought and play what many of us identify as a self? Is it our felt version of Descartes's *Cogito, ergo sum*?

In *The Principles of Psychology*, Henry James's older brother, William, develops a broad notion of self or selves that begins with the body of a person, a material self, a *Me*, which then moves outward to include a wider self—the *Mine*, which embraces a man's clothes, his family, his home and property, his successes and failures. Notably, James acknowledges that parts of our bodies are more intimate than others, that a lot of self-feeling—or what he calls "the Self of Selves"—happens "between the head and throat,"[190] or from the neck up, not the neck down. In light of this fluctuating self, James makes a distinction between the unsympathetic and the sympathetic person. Using Stoicism as an example of the unsympathetic character, he argues, "All narrow people retrench their Me, they retract it,—from the region of what they cannot securely possess."[191] Sympathetic characters, on the other hand, "proceed by the entirely opposite way of expansion and inclusion. The outline of their self often gets uncertain enough, but for this the spread of its content more than atones."[192] James's conception of self is elastic—it shrinks and grows depending on one's personality and from moment to moment in a single person's life. It might be because the outline of my self is subject to some blur that I lean in the sympathetic direction, that I like the idea that we both take in the world and move outward toward it, and that movement is part of a feeling of my *self* that includes others. I am not always locked away in the cell of my private, hidden thoughts, and even when I am, large parts of my world are closed in with me—chattering multitudes.

We cannot uncover "a frozen universe of objects independent of all gaze and thought," but there is an intersubjective world of shared languages, images, reason, and other people, and I do think that greater or lesser openness to those words and pictures and persons is possible. Some people have tight, hard little selves. Others are more open. Some are so open they drown in other people, like the psychiatric patients who confuse "I" and "you." Nevertheless, there are moments when I find myself lost in you. There are also moments when I look so hard at a thing that I disappear.

The internal narrator takes a holiday, leaves me for a while. Actions and words continually confound this narrator, not only in the form of roaming alien hands, flashbacks, seizures, and visual or auditory hallucinations but also in far more mundane events. I find my fingers moving toward the bowl of chocolates before I *know* they are doing it, or a sentence fragment or melody arrives unbidden in my head. How many times have I met a person and instantly felt something was wrong? It was not through verbal communication that I understood this. Before I am able to articulate the problem to myself, I feel it. Later, I might speculate that perhaps I sensed a stiffness in the other person's body, which then registered in my own, or saw him glance elsewhere, and that look reverberated in my chest or registered itself as a tightening around my own eyes or an inadvertent movement backward. Mirror-touch synesthesia or not, I am surely not alone. We respond to what is beyond our own bodies with feeling that is prere-flective, an embodied meaning. That feeling is conscious surely, but not "hero of my own life" self-conscious. I am not looking at myself feeling.

THE CONSCIOUS SELF'S BOUNDARIES SHIFT. It is a ques-tion of ownership, of me and mine. A patient in the neuro-logy ward with damage to her right hemisphere neglects her paralyzed left arm for a week, insisting that it belongs to her doctor. Her physician may tell her that she has it wrong, it's her arm, but she will not believe it. But then, in time, she comes to understand that the limb is hers. She is able to re-claim it, although an underground part of her has always known that it is hers, and she can't move the miserable thing. What has changed? Did the truth of her paralysis suddenly enter her consciousness? Can she say, "I now remember that my arm is useless"? One day, after eight long years, Justine Etchevery is able to take back the use of her arms and legs. She wants to walk, and she does. She regains a sense of willed movement: *I can walk.* What jogged that miracle? Did an unconscious idea of her paralysis suddenly dissolve, one that we could now see on a scan as a vanished asymmetry in her brain? The veteran of the First World War cannot hear or speak until one day his body erupts in spasms and his hearing and speech return. He is able to say, "I can hear, I can speak." I don't know whether he could then remember and tell the story of what happened to him in the trench. But I know that telling is not enough. The meaning of what happened to him would have to be felt and recognized as his or it would be nonsense. Anna Freud was the first to use the word *intellectualize* to describe people who use verbal ideas as a form of defense. A patient talks about his mother's suicide as a clinical story of her depression and tells it without feeling or affect, in a calm, neutral recitation that should be connected to emotion but has become removed from it. He, too, has *la belle indifférence.* The shattering loss is kept at a distance; its meaning goes unrecognized because to see it is terrifying. And then, after the back-and-forth of psychotherapy, during which he reflects and is reflected back upon himself through the eyes of his analyst, he senses a change, a new configuration of his consciousness that includes both knowing and feeling. He retells the story, and in the retelling, which is also a reinvention, he feels the undercurrents and rhythms of his lived body. He makes the wrenching loss his own in an act of creative memory; it becomes part of his narrative self. And there are neuronal changes in his brain accordingly, in the limbic emotional systems and the prefrontal executive areas. There are times when we all resist claiming what should be ours; it is alien, and we do not want to take it into the stories we spin about ourselves.

Clearly, a self is much larger than the internal narrator. Around and beneath the island of that self-conscious storyteller is a vast sea of unconsciousness, of what we don't know, will never know, or have forgotten. There is much in us we don't control or will, but that doesn't mean that making a narrative for ourselves is unimportant. In language we represent the passage of time as we sense it—the *was,* the *is,* the *will be.* We abstract and we think and we tell. We order our memories and link them together, and those disparate fragments gain an owner: the "I" of autobiography, who is no one without a "you." For whom do we narrate, after all? Even when alone in our heads, there is a presumed other, the second person of our speech. Can a story ever be true? There will always be holes in it, the unarticulated breaches in our understanding, which we leap over with an "and" or a "then" or a "later." But that is the route to coherence.

Coherence cannot eliminate ambiguity, however. Ambiguity is not quite one thing, not quite the other. It won't fit into the pigeonhole, the neat box, the window frame, the encyclopedia. It is a formless object or feeling that can't be placed. Ambiguity asks, Where is the border between this and that? Ambiguity does not obey logic. The logician says, "To tolerate contradiction is to be indifferent to truth." Those particular philosophers like to play games of true and false. It is one or the other, never both. But ambiguity is inherently contradictory and insoluble, a bewildering truth of fogs and mists and the unrecognizable figure or phantom or memory or dream that cannot be contained or held in my hands because it is always flying away, and I can't tell what it is or if it is anything at all. I chase it with words even though it won't be captured and, every once in a while, I imagine I have come close to it. In May of 2006, I stood outside under a cloudless blue sky and started to speak about my father, who had been dead for over two years. As soon as I opened my mouth, I began to shake violently. I shook that day and then I shook again on other days. I am the shaking woman.

NOTES

1. Owsei Temkin, *The Falling Sickness: A History of Epilepsy from the Greeks to the Beginnings of Modern Neurology*, 2nd ed. (Baltimore: Johns Hopkins Press, 1971), 36.
2. Frances Hill, *The Salem Witch Trials Reader* (New York: Da Capo Press, 2000), 59.
3. Temkin, *Falling Sickness*, 194.
4. Ibid., 225.
5. *Diagnostic Statistical Manual of Mental Disorders*, 4th ed. (Arlington, VA: American Psychiatric Association, 2000), 492–98. Hereafter *DSM-IV*.
6. Ibid., 493.
7. Carl W. Basil, *Living Well with Epilepsy and Other Seizure Disorders* (New York: Harper Resource, 2004), 73.
8. J. Lindsay Allet and Rachel E. Allet, "Somatoform Disorders in Neurological Practice," *Current Opinion in Psychiatry* 19 (2006): 413–20.
9. "Introduction," *DSM-IV*, xxx.
10. Peter Rudnytsky, *Reading Psychoanalysis: Freud, Rank, Ferenczi, Groddeck* (Ithaca: Cornell University Press, 2002), 90.

bert J. Campbell, *Campbell's Psychiatric Dictionary*, 8th ed. (Oxford: Oxford University Press, 2004), 189.

12. Sigmund Freud and Josef Breuer, *Studies on Hysteria*, trans. James Strachey (New York: Basic Books, 1957), 86.

13. Sigmund Freud, *On Aphasia: A Critical Study*, trans. E. Stengel (New York: International Universities Press, 1953), 55.

14. George Makari, *Revolution in Mind: The Creation of Psychoanalysis* (New York: HarperCollins, 2008), 70.

15. Freud and Breuer, *Studies on Hysteria*, 160–61.

16. Christopher G. Goetz, Michel Bonduelle, and Toby Gelfand, *Charcot: Constructing Neurology* (Oxford: Oxford University Press, 1995), 172–213.

17. Pierre Janet, *The Major Symptoms of Hysteria: Fifteen Lectures Given in the Medical School of Harvard University* (London: Macmillan, 1907), 324.

18. Ibid., 332.

19. Ibid., 325–26.

20. Ibid., 42.

21. Ibid., 38.

22. Eugene C. Toy and Debra Klamen, *Case Files: Psychiatry* (New York: McGraw-Hill, 2004), 401.

23. Todd Feinberg, *Altered Egos: How the Brain Creates the Self* (Oxford: Oxford University Press, 2001), 28.

24. Rita Charon, *Narrative Medicine: Honoring the Stories of Illness* (Oxford: Oxford University Press, 2006), 9.

25. J.-K. Zubieta et al., "Placebo Effects Mediated by Endogenous Opioid Activity on μ-Opioid Receptors," *Journal of Neuroscience* 25 (2005): 7754–62.

26. Erika Kinetz, "Is Hysteria Real? Brain Images Say Yes," *New York Times*, Sept. 26, 2006.

27. Sean A. Spence, "All in the Mind? The Neural Correlates of Unexplained Physical Symptoms," *Advances in Psychiatric Treatment* 12 (2006): 357.

28. Goetz, Bonduelle, and Gelfand, *Charcot*, 192.

29. P. Vuilleumier et al., "Functional Neuroanatomical Correlates of Hysterical Sensorimotor Loss," *Brain* 124, no. 6 (June 2001): 1077.

30. Quoted in Goetz, Bonduelle, Gelfand, *Charcot*, 187.

31. Freud and Breuer, *Studies on Hysteria*, 7.

32. Bertram G. Katzung, ed., *Basic and Clinical Pharmacology*, 9th ed. (New York: Lange Medical Books / McGraw-Hill, 2004), 156.

33. James L. McGaugh, *Memory and Emotion: The Making of Lasting Memories* (New York: Columbia University Press, 2003), 93.

34. Ibid., 107

35. Quoted in Daniel Brown, Alan W. Scheflin, and D. Corydon Hammond, *Memory, Trauma, Treatment and the Law* (New York: Norton, 1998), 95.

36. Françoise Davoine and Jean-Max Gaudillière, *History Beyond Trauma*, trans. Susan Fairfield (New York: Other Press, 2004), 179.

37. Onno van der Hart, Ellert R. S. Nijenhuis, and Kathy Steele, *The Haunted*

Self: Structural Dissociation and the Treatment of Chronic Trauma (New York: Norton, 2006).

38. Ian Hacking, *Rewriting the Soul: Multiple Personality and the Sciences of Memory* (Princeton, NJ : Princeton University Press, 1995), 21.
39. Janet, *Major Symptoms*, 131.
40. Ibid., 172.
41. *Three Short Novels of Dostoyevsky*, trans. Constance Garnett, ed. Avrahm Yarmolinsky (New York: Doubleday, 1960), 15.
42. Hans Christian Andersen, "The Shadow," in *Fairy Tales*, vol. 2, trans. R. P. Keigwin (Odense, Denmark: Hans Reitzels Forlag, 1985), 188.
43. Klaus Podoll and Markus Dahlem, http://www.migraine-aura.org. See also P. Brugger, M. Regard, and T. Landis, "Illusory Replication of One's Own Body: Phenomenology and Classification of Autoscopic Phenomena," *Cognitive Neuropsychiatry* 2, no. 1 (1997): 19–38.
44. Todd Feinberg and Raymond M. Shapiro, "Misidentification-Reduplication and the Right Hemisphere," *Neuropsychiatry, Neuropsychology and Behavioral Neurology* (2, no. 1): 39–48.
45. Feinberg, *Altered Egos*, 74–75.
46. Jacques Lacan, "The Mirror Stage as Formative of the I Function," in *Écrits*, trans. Bruce Fink (New York: Norton, 2006), 75–81.
47. Maurice Merleau-Ponty, "The Child's Relation to Others," *The Primacy of Perception*, trans. William Cobb (Chicago: Northwestern University Press, 1964), 117.
48. Shaun Gallagher, *How the Body Shapes the Mind* (Oxford: Clarendon Press, 2005), 26.
49. Roger W. Sperry, "Some Effects of Disconnecting the Cerebral Hemispheres," *Bioscience Reports* 2, no. 5 (May 1982): 267.
50. Dahlia W. Zaidel, "A View of the World from a Split-Brain Perspective," http://cogprints.org/920/0/critchelyf.pdf.
51. Quoted in Feinberg, *Altered Egos*, 94.
52. Mark Solms and Oliver Turnbull, *The Brain and the Inner World* (New York: Other Press, 2002), 82.
53. M. S. Gazzaniga, J. E. LeDoux, and D. H. Wilson, "Language, Praxis, and the Right Hemisphere: Clues to Some Mechanisms of Consciousness," *Neurology* 27 (1977): 1144–47.
54. A. R. Luria and F. I. Yudovich, *Speech and the Development of Mental Processes in the Child* (Harmondsworth, UK: Penguin, 1971).
55. Davoine and Gaudillière, 115.
56. A. R. Luria, *Higher Cortical Functions in Man*, trans. Basil Haigh, 2nd ed. (New York: Basic Books, 1962), 32.
57. Sigmund Freud, *Beyond the Pleasure Principle*, trans. James Strachey (New York: Norton, 1961), 9.
58. Freud and Breuer, *Studies on Hysteria*, 49.
59. Ibid., 44.

60. Sigmund Freud, *The Ego and the Id,* trans. James Strachey (1923; repr., New York: Norton, 1960), 32–33.

61. Charles Dickens, *David Copperfield* (1850; repr., Oxford: Oxford University Press, 2000), 1.

62. Joe Brainard, *I Remember* (New York: Penguin, 1975), 28. Joe Brainard is known chiefly as a visual artist. He was part of the group of writers and painters known as the New York School, which included John Ashbery, Fairfield Porter, Alex Katz, Kenward Elmslie, Frank O'Hara, James Schuyler, Kenneth Koch, and Rudy Burkhardt. His work is in the Museum of Modern Art and the Whitney Museum. He died in 1994. *I Remember* inspired the French writer Georges Perec to do his own version of this memory-generating machine: *Je Me Souviens.*

63. Faraneh Vargha-Khadem, Elizabeth Isaacs, and Mortimer Mishkin, "Agnosia, Alexia and a Remarkable form of Amnesia in an Adolescent Boy," *Brain* 117, no. 4 (1994), 683–703.

64. Ibid., 698.

65. Charles D. Fox, *Psychopathology of Hysteria* (Boston: Gorham Press, 1913), 58.

66. A. R. Luria, *The Man with a Shattered World,* trans. Lynn Solotaroff (Cambridge, MA: Harvard University Press, 1972), 92.

67. Quoted in Elaine Showalter, *Hystories: Hysterical Epidemics and Modern Culture* (London: Picador, 1998), 34.

68. Georges Didi-Huberman, *Invention of Hysteria: Charcot and the Photographic Iconography of the Salpêtrière,* trans. Alisa Hartz (Cambridge, MA: MIT Press, 2003).

69. Alan B. Ettinger and Andres M. Kanner, *Psychiatric Issues in Epilepsy: A Practical Guide to Diagnosis and Treatment,* 2nd ed. (Philadelphia: Lippincott, Williams & Wilkins, 2007), 471–72.

70. *DSM-IV,* 494.

71. Ibid., 496.

72. The experiences of soldiers with conversion disorder may shed light on one of the reasons women may be more vulnerable to hysteria than men outside of combat situations. If powerlessness and a feeling of having no active role in your fate are linked to the illness, then it makes sense that women, who have traditionally had far less autonomy than men, would suffer in higher numbers. Similarly, in many reference books, including the *DSM,* there is repeated speculation that hysteria is more common in uneducated people from developing societies, which seems to be another way of saying that people who feel their will is undermined by forces they don't control may be more likely to succumb to a conversion.

73. C. S. Myers, *Shellshock in France 1914–18* (Cambridge: Cambridge University Press, 1940), 42–43.

74. Edwin A. Weinstein, "Conversion Disorders," http://www.bordeninstitute .army.mil/published_volumes/war_psychiatry/WarPsychChapter15.pdf, 385.

75. R. J. Heruti et al., "Conversion Motor Paralysis Disorder: Analysis of 34 Consecutive Referrals," *Spinal Cord* 40, no. 7 (July 2002): 335–40.
76. *DSM-IV*, 467.
77. Trevor H. Hurwitz and James W. Pritchard, "Conversion Disorder and fMRI," *Neurology* 67 (2006): 1914–15.
78. Goetz, Bonduelle, and Gelfand, *Charcot*, 178–79.
79. K. M. Yazici and L. Kostakoglu, "Cerebral Blood Flow Changes in Patients with Conversion Disorder," *Psychiatry Research: Neuroimaging* 83, no. 3 (1998): 166.
80. Vuilleumier et al., "Functional Neuroanatomical Correlates," 1082.
81. D. W. Winnicott, *Home Is Where We Start From: Essays by a Psychoanalyst* (New York: Norton, 1986), 32.
82. Vuilleumier et al., "Functional Neuroanatomical Correlates," 1082.
83. Gallagher, *How the Body Shapes the Mind*, 41.
84. Karen Kaplan-Solms and Mark Solms, *Clinical Studies in Neuro-Psychoanalysis: Introduction to a Depth Neuropsychology* (New York: Karnac, 2002), 151–52.
85. Ibid., 190–91.
86. Ibid., 177.
87. Benjamin Libet, "Do We Have Free Will?" *Journal of Consciousness Studies* 6, no. 8–9 (1999): 47–57.
88. Julian Offray de La Mettrie, *Machine Man and Other Writings*, trans. and ed. Ann Thompson (Cambridge: Cambridge University Press, 1996).
89. Jaak Panksepp, *Affective Neuroscience: The Foundations of Human and Animal Emotions* (Oxford: Oxford University Press, 1998), 52.
90. Antonio Damasio, *Descartes' Error: Emotion, Reason and the Human Brain* (New York: HarperCollins, 2000), 3–79.
91. William James, *The Will to Believe and Other Essays in Popular Philosophy* (1897; repr., New York: Barnes and Noble Books, 2005), 92.
92. Edmund Husserl, *Ideas Pertaining to a Pure Phenomenology and to a Phenomenological Philosophy, Second Book*, trans. R. Rojcewicz and A. Schuwer (Dordrecht: Kluwer, 1989), 19–20. I have simplified Husserl. We all have both *Körper*, a sense of our material selves, and *Leib*, an inner living awareness, but this distinction is enough to serve my purpose here. It seems clear, however, that in sickness the body becomes more thinglike. Its reality as not only *Leib* but also *Körper* is brought home.
93. D. W. Winnicott, "Mirror-Role of Mother and Family in Child Development," in *Playing and Reality* (London: Routledge, 1989), 111.
94. Ibid., 112.
95. Ibid., 114.
96. Quoted in Allan Schore, *Affect Regulation and the Origin of the Self: The Neurobiology of Emotional Development* (Hillsdale, NJ: Lawrence Erlbaum, 1994), 76.
97. Ibid., 91.

98. Gallagher, *How the Body Shapes the Mind*, 73. Gallagher is strongly influenced by Merleau-Ponty, who in turn was influenced by Husserl. Husserl argues that we have a subjective conscious sense of our freedom to move, but that "the appearances that are arriving are already prefigured. The appearances form dependent systems. Only as dependent on kinaestheses can they continually pass into one another and constitute a unity of one sense." The conscious is linked to a kinetic/motor bodily unconsciousness. See "Horizons and the Genesis of Perception" in *The Essential Husserl: Basic Writings in Transcendental Phenomenology*, ed. Donn Welton (Bloomington: Indiana University Press, 1999), 227–28.

99. V. Gallese, L. Fadiga, L. Fogassi, and G. Rizzolatti, "Action Recognition in the Premotor Cortex," *Brain* 119 (1996): 593–609. Gallese's ongoing research into the neurobiology of intersubjectivity is an interdisciplinary one that draws from psychology and philosophy as well as science. For an illuminating discussion of his position that intersubjectivity is primarily a prerational, embodied reality, also called intercorporeity, see Vittorio Gallese, "The Two Sides of Mimesis: Girard's Mimetic Theory, Embodied Simulation and Social Identification," *Journal of Consciousness Studies* 16, no. 4 (2009), 21–44.

100. G. W. F. Hegel, *The Phenomenology of Mind*, trans. J. B. Baillie, 2nd ed. (London: Allen and Unwin, 1949), 232.

101. Merleau-Ponty, "Child's Relation to Others," 151.

102. Margarite Sechehaye, *Autobiography of a Schizophrenic Girl: The True Story of Renee*, trans. Grace Rubin-Rabson (New York: Penguin, 1994), 52–53.

103. Quoted in J. Laplanche and J. B. Pontalis, *The Language of Psychoanalysis*, trans. Donald Nicholson-Smith (New York: Norton, 1973), 199.

104. Leo Tolstoy, "The Death of Iván Ilých," in *Great Short Works of Leo Tolstoy*, trans. Louise Maude and Aylmer Maude (New York: Harper & Row, 1967), 280.

105. Ibid., 282.

106. Albertus Magnus, "Commentary on Aristotle," "On Memory and Recollection," *The Medieval Craft of Memory: An Anthology of Texts and Pictures*, ed. Mary Carruthers and Jan M. Ziolkowski (Philadelphia: University of Pennsylvania Press, 2002), 153–188.

107. A. R. Luria. *The Mind of a Mnemonist: A Little Book About a Vast Memory*, trans. Lynn Solotaroff (Cambridge, MA: Harvard University Press, 1987), 32.

108. Quoted in Patricia Lynne Duffy, *Blue Cats and Chartreuse Kittens: How Synesthetes Color Their World* (New York: Henry Holt, 2001), 22.

109. Arthur Rimbaud, *Complete Works*, trans. Paul Schmidt (New York: Harper & Row, 1967), 123.

110. Luria, *Mind of a Mnemonist*, 31.

111. Jorge Luis Borges, "Funes the Memorious," *Labyrinths: Selected Stories and Other Writings* (New York: New Directions, 1964), 65–67.

112. Luria, *Mind of a Mnemonist*, 154.

113. Ibid., 155.

114. Freud used *Nachträglichkeit*, deferred action, throughout his writing, from 1896, in a letter to his friend Fliess, onward. For a clear account of this complex term and why deferred action might not be the best translation, see Laplanche and Pontalis, *Language of Psychoanalysis*, 111–14.

115. Joseph LeDoux, *Synaptic Self: How Our Brains Become Who We Are* (New York: Penguin, 2002), 124.

116. Demis Hassabis, Dharshan Kumaran, Seralynne D. Vann, and Eleanor Maguire, "Patients with Hippocampal Amnesia Cannot Imagine New Experiences," *Proceedings of the National Academy of Sciences* 104 (2007): 1726–31.

117. LeDoux, *Synaptic Self*, 217.

118. Francis Crick, *The Astonishing Hypothesis: The Scientific Search for the Soul* (New York: Simon & Schuster, 1995), 3.

119. LeDoux, *Synaptic Self*, 94.

120. S. J. Blakemore, D. Bristow, G. Bird, C. Frith, and J. Ward, "Somatosensory Activations Following the Observation of Touch and a Case of Vision Touch Synesthesia," *Brain* 128 (2005): 1571–83; and Michael J. Banissy and Jamie Ward, "Mirror Touch Synesthesia Is Linked to Empathy," *Nature Neuroscience* 10 (2007): 815–16.

121. Luria, *Mind of a Mnemonist*, 82.

122. Duffy, *Blue Cats*, 33.

123. See Peter Brugger, "Reflective Mirrors: Perspective-Taking in Autoscopic Phenomenon," *Cognitive Neuropsychiatry* 7 (2002): 188.

124. K. Hitomi, "'Transitional Subject' in Two Cases of Psychotherapy of Schizophrenia," *Schweizer Archiv für Neurologie und Psychiatrie* 153, no. 1 (2002), 39–41.

125. Ibid., 40.

126. Winnicott, *Playing and Reality*, 2.

127. Freud, *Mourning and Melancholia*, Standard Edition, vol. 14, trans. James Strachey (London: Hogarth Press, 1957).

128. After reading the manuscript of this book, a friend of mine who is also a psychoanalyst pointed out that to have a lump in one's throat means sadness.

129. Theodore Roethke, "Silence," *Collected Poems* (New York: Doubleday, 1966).

130. Sigmund Freud, *The Interpretation of Dreams*, Standard Edition, vol. 4, trans. James Strachey (London: Hogarth Press, 1953, 1971), 279.

131. Cited in Mark Solms, "Dreaming and REM Sleep Are Controlled by Different Brain Mechanisms," *Sleep and Dreaming: Scientific Advances and Reconsiderations* (Cambridge: Cambridge University Press, 2003), 52.

132. J. Allan Hobson, *Dreaming: An Introduction to the Science of Sleep* (Oxford: Oxford University Press, 2002), 155–56.

133. Antti Revonsuo, "The Reinterpretation of Dreams: An Evolutionary Hypothesis of the Function of Dreaming," *Sleep and Dreaming*, 89.

134. Ibid., 94.

135. Solms, *Sleep and Dreaming*, 56.

136. *Dream Debate: Hobson vs. Solms—Should Freud's Dream Theory Be Abandoned?*, DVD, NetiNeti Media, 2006. For another view that disagrees with both Hobson and Solms, see G. W. Domhoff, "Refocusing the Neurocognitive Approach to Dreams: A Critique of the Hobson Versus Solms Debate," *Dreaming* 15 (2005): 3–20.

137. William James, *Pragmatism*. In *Writings 1902–1910* (New York: Library of America, 1987), 491.

138. For a brief discussion of color as a prereflective phenomenon, see Kym Maclaren, "Embodied Perceptions of Others as a Condition of Selfhood," *Journal of Consciousness Studies* 15, no. 8 (2008): 75.

139. The Mary story has been told and retold in many different papers, books, and lectures. For an argument against the Mary story as a proof of qualia, see Daniel Dennett, *Consciousness Explained* (Boston: Little, Brown, 1991), 398–401.

140. Ned Block's interview is in Susan Blakemore, *Conversations on Consciousness* (Oxford: Oxford University Press, 2005), 24–35.

141. Peter Carruthers's paper, published in the *Journal of Philosophy*, was sent to me by the "sympathetic" philosopher Ned Block after I had heard the lecture on theories of consciousness he gave in February 2009 at the New York Psychoanalytic Institute in New York City. "Brute Experience," *Journal of Philosophy* 86 (1989): 258–69.

142. Ludwig Wittgenstein, *Tractatus Logico-Philosophicus*, trans. D. F. Pears and B. F. McGuinness (London: Routledge & Kegan Paul, 1963), 151.

143. Simone de Beauvoir, *Philosophical Writings*, ed. Margaret A. Simons (Urbana: University of Illinois Press, 2004), 159.

144. For a useful introduction to Patricia Churchland's view of the mind, as well as those of several other prominent neuroscientists and philosophers, see Blakemore, *Conversations on Consciousness*.

145. Francisco J. Varela, Evan Thompson, and Eleanor Rosch, *The Embodied Mind: Cognitive Science and the Human Experience* (Cambridge, MA: MIT Press, 1993).

146. The physicist Erwin Schrodinger offers a view of consciousness that draws insights from the Upanishads and Schopenhauer in a remarkable, if neglected little book published after his death. Erwin Schrodinger, *My View of the World*, trans. Cecily Hastings (Woodbridge, Conn: Ox Bow Press, 1983). On page 88 he gives us the colors he associates with vowels, writing about his synesthesia as a common phenomenon: "For me they are a—pale mid-brown, e—white, i—intense, brilliant blue, o—black, u—chocolate brown."

147. Jan-Markus Schwindt, "Mind as Hardware and Matter as Software," *Journal of Consciousness Studies* 15, no. 4 (2008): 22–23.

148. George Berkeley, *The Principles of Human Knowledge*, pt. 1, *Berkeley's Philosophical Writings*, ed. David M. Armstrong (New York: Collier, 1965), 63.

149. Schwindt, "Mind as Hardware," 25.
150. Imants Baruss, "Beliefs About Consciousness and Reality," *Journal of Consciousness Studies* 15, no. 10–11 (2008): 287.
151. D. Berman and W. Lyons, "J. B. Watson's Rejection of Mental Images," *Journal of Consciousness Studies* 14, no. 11 (2007): 24.
152. Steven C. Schachter, Gregory Holmes, and Dorthée G. A. Kasteleijn-Nolst Trenité, *Behavioral Aspects of Epilepsy: Principles and Practice* (New York: Demos, 2008), 471.
153. Ibid., 472.
154. Oliver Sacks, *Migraine: Understanding a Common Disorder* (Berkeley: University of California Press, 1985), 104.
155. Ibid., 104.
156. Alan B. Ettinger and Andres M. Kanner, *Psychiatric Issues in Epilepsy: A Practical Guide to Diagnosis and Treatment,* 2nd ed. (Philadelphia: Lippincott, Williams & Wilkens, 2007), 286–88.
157. Schacter, Holmes, and Kasteleijn-Nolst Trenité, *Behavioral Aspects of Epilepsy,* 210.
158. Steve Connor, " 'God Spot' Is Found in Brain," *Los Angeles Times,* Oct. 29, 1997; and "Doubt Cast over Brain God Spot," *BBC News,* Aug. 30, 2006. Two studies about religion and the brain resulted in wide media attention. The first, conducted at the University of California, San Diego, in 1997 (by V. S. Ramachandran et al.), was done on people with temporal lobe epilepsy, people who admitted to being highly religious, and normal controls. The scientists tested their subjects' galvanic skin response (GSR) and found strong emotional responses to spiritual words in the epileptics and the religious but not the normals. Ramachandran speculated that temporal lobe as well as limbic activity creates greater religiosity. See V. S. Ramachandran and Sandra Blakeslee, *Phantoms in the Brain: Probing the Mysteries of the Human Mind* (New York: William Morrow, 1997), 174–98. The second study, done in Canada by Mario Beauregard, gave fMRIs to fifteen Carmelite nuns and found no such localization: "Mystical experiences are mediated by several brain regions." The researchers did find, however, that "right medial temporal activation was related to a subjective experience of contacting a spiritual reality." M. Beauregard and V. Paquette, "Neural Correlates of Mystical Experiences in Carmelite Nuns," *Neuroscience Letters* 405 (2006): 186–90. It is only fair to point out that the scientists involved are more circumspect about their findings than the journalists who report on them. Nevertheless, philosophical confusion is often rampant. Michael A. Persinger has worked extensively in the field of mystical experience and temporal lobe activation, but he also links these transcendent experiences to early child-parent relations. See his book *Neuropsychological Bases of God Beliefs* (New York: Praeger Publishers, 1987).
159. Sigmund Freud, *Civilization and Its Discontents,* Standard Edition, vol. 21, trans. James Strachey (London: Hogarth Press, 1957), 64.

160. S. G. Waxman and N. Geschwind, "The Interictal Behavior Syndrome in Temporal Lobe Epilepsy," *Archives of General Psychiatry* 32 (1975): 1580–86.

161. Many books contain speculative diagnoses of the famous. See J. Bogousslavsky and F. Boller, eds., *Neurological Disorders in Famous Artists*, vol. 19 (Lausanne: Karger, 2005); and Frank Clifford Rose, ed., *Neurology of the Arts: Painting, Music, Literature* (London: Imperial College Press, 2004). For a popular account that liberally identifies innumerable notables of the recent and distant past as temporal lobe epileptics, see Eve LaPlante, *Seized: Temporal Lobe Epilepsy as a Medical, Historical, and Artistic Phenomenon* (Lincoln, NE: Authors Guild Backinprint.com, 1993).

162. Gershom Scholem, *Major Trends in Jewish Mysticism* (New York: Schocken, 1961), 151.

163. William James, *Varieties of Religious Experience* (1902; repr., New York: Library of America, 1987), 23.

164. Fyodor Dostoyevsky, *The Idiot*, trans. David Magarshack (New York: Penguin, 1955), 258–59.

165. Saint Augustine, *Confessions*, trans. Henry Chadwick (Oxford: Oxford University Press, 1988), 152.

166. Julian Jaynes, *The Origin of Consciousness in the Breakdown of the Bicameral Mind* (Boston: Houghton Mifflin, 1976).

167. Marcel Kuijsten, ed., *Reflections on the Dawn of Consciousness: Julian Jaynes's Bicameral Mind Theory Revisited* (Henderson, NV: Julian Jaynes Society, 2006), 119–21.

168. Schore, *Affect Regulation*, 488.

169. Cited in Kristen I. Taylor and Marianne Regard, "Language in the Right Cerebral Hemisphere: Contributions from Reading Studies," *News in Physiological Sciences* 18, no. 6 (2003): 258.

170. Julia Kane, "Poetry as Right-Hemispheric Language," *Journal of Consciousness Studies* 11, no. 5–6 (2004), 21–59.

171. Daniel Smith, *Muses, Madmen and Prophets: Rethinking the History, Science, and Meaning of Auditory Hallucinations* (New York: Penguin, 2007), 136–140.

172. Simone Weil, *Gravity and Grace*, trans. Arthur Wills (1952; repr., Lincoln: University of Nebraska Press, 1997), 51.

173. Patrick Wall, *Pain: The Science of Suffering* (New York: Columbia University Press, 2000), 63.

174. Ludwig Wittgenstein, *Philosophical Investigations*, 2nd ed. (New York: Macmillan, 1958), 102e.

175. According to one source, there have been about three thousand studies conducted on the relative effectiveness of psychotherapy and medication for clinical depression. Early research that paved the way for following investigations was done by the National Institute of Mental Health's Treatment of Depression Collaborative Research Program (Elkin et al., 1985, 1989; Weisman et al., 1986), which demonstrated that various kinds of psychological therapies were as effective in treating depression as antidepressants. This has

been borne out by many studies since, especially in cases of mild and moderate depression. In one, the authors found considerable improvement in people who used either a drug or some form of psychotherapy for depression, but their research also concluded that combining antidepressants with psychotherapy had a lower rate of treatment failure than either drugs or therapy alone and resulted in fewer hospitalizations and better work adjustment among the patients. Burnand et al., "Psychodynamic Psychotherapy and Clomipramine in the Treatment of Major Depression," *Psychiatric Services* 53, no. 5 (2002): 585–90. For more recent research comparing drugs and psychotherapies, see Cuijpers et al., "Are Psychological and Pharmacological Interventions Equally Effective in the Treatment of Adult Depressive Disorders? A Meta-analysis of Comparative Studies," *Journal of Clinical Psychiatry* 69, no. 11 (2008): 1675–85. There is also growing research on neurobiological changes induced by psychotherapy. See Etkin et al., "Toward a Neurobiology of Psychotherapy," *Journal of Neuropsychiatry and Clinical Neurosciences* 17 (2005): 145–58; as well as Henn et al., "Psychotherapy and Antidepressant Treatment: Evidence for Similar Neurobiological Mechanisms," *World Psychiatry* 1, no. 2 (2002).

176. Merleau-Ponty, "Child's Relation to Others," 163.
177. Mary Douglas, *Purity and Danger* (London: Routledge & Kegan Paul, 1966), 95.
178. Ian Hacking, *The Social Construction of What?* (Cambridge, MA: Harvard University Press, 1999), 123.
179. For a good introduction to Habermas, see *The Philosophical Discourses of Modernity: Twelve Lectures,* trans. Frederick G. Lawrence (Cambridge, MA: MIT Press, 1990). Habermas does not believe that we can jump out of our own heads and become objective observers of the world. He does believe in reason and reasonable discourse as a way to arrive at consensus. His view of science and technology is complex. He argues that human beings can apply what he calls "Technical Cognitive Interest," technical rules of understanding, which, through their use, extend human control over nature. See Jürgen Habermas, *Theory and Practice,* trans. John Viertel (Boston: Beacon Press, 1973), 142–69.
180. G. Alacón et al., "Is It Worth Pursuing Surgery for Epilepsy in Patients with Normal Neuroimaging?" *Journal of Neurology, Neurosurgery, and Psychiatry,* 77 (2006): 474–80.
181. Oliver Sacks, "Witty Ticky Ray," *The Man Who Mistook His Wife for a Hat* (New York: Summit Books, 1995), 92–101.
182. Alice W. Flaherty, *The Midnight Disease: The Drive to Write, Writer's Block, and the Creative Brain* (Boston: Houghton Mifflin, 2004), 234.
183. Panksepp, *Affective Neuroscience,* 311–13.
184. Antonio Damasio, *The Feeling of What Happens: Body and Emotion in the Making of Consciousness* (San Diego: Harvest Harcourt, 1999), 134–43.
185. Michael S. Gazzaniga, *Nature's Mind: The Biological Roots of Thinking, Emotions, Sexuality, Language and Intelligence* (New York: Basic Books, 1992), 2.

186. Stephen Pinker, *The Blank Slate: The Modern Denial of Human Nature* (New York: Viking, 2002).

187. For an intelligent discussion of innateness versus learning, see LeDoux's comments on the subject in *Synaptic Self*, 82–93. There is a vast body of scientific literature on the effects of maternal nurture, as well as maternal separation, on offspring that is not cited by Pinker. The subjects of these studies run the gamut from rats and mice to primates and human beings. For a collection of eighty-two papers from researchers in various but related disciplines, see John T. Cacioppo et al., eds., *Foundations in Social Neuroscience* (Cambridge, MA: MIT Press, 2002). Included are neurobiological studies on rats that specifically address the question of genetic and environmental interaction: Liu et al., "Maternal Care, Hippocampal Glucocortoid Receptors, and Hypothalamic-Pituitary-Andrenal Response to Stress"; and Francis et al., "Nongenomic Transmission Across Generations of Maternal Behavior and Stress Response in the Rat." See also Jaak Panksepp's discussion of the brain systems for social attachment and separation distress in *Affective Neuroscience*. There is a burgeoning literature of research on infant and child attachment, a field pioneered by John Bowlby in his three-volume masterwork *Attachment and Loss* (New York: Basic Books, 1969).

188. D. W. Winnicott, "Ego Distortion in Terms of True and False Self," in *The Maturational Processes and the Facilitating Environment* (London: Karnac, 1990), 140–52.

189. Henry James, *What Maisie Knew* (Oxford: Oxford University Press, 1996), 22–23.

190. William James, *The Principles of Psychology* (1892; repr., Chicago: Encyclopaedia Britannica, 1952), 194.

191. Ibid., 201.

192. Ibid., 202.

ACKNOWLEDGMENTS

This book began with a talk I gave at New York Presbyterian Hospital as part of a series of Grand Rounds lectures hosted by Columbia University's Program in Narrative Medicine. Rita Charon, the director of the program, invited me to speak. Her enthusiasm and generosity about what I had to say acted as a vital catalyst for this book. The now-disbanded neuropsychoanalysis discussion group I attended for two years, led by Jaak Panksepp and the late Mortimer Ostow, not only introduced me to the vast field of neuroscience research, it allowed me to listen to (and sometimes participate in) the complex debates that surround the integration of two disciplines that have entirely different vocabularies. The neuroscience lectures, hosted by the Neuropsychoanalysis Foundation at the New York Psychoanalytic Institute, were crucial to increasing my understanding and inspiring directions for my reading. I want to thank Dahelia Beverle, my supervisor at the Payne Whitney Psychiatric Clinic in New York City, where I volunteer as a writing teacher for the in-patients. The writers in my classes provided me with invaluable insights about the personal meanings of their illnesses, without which this book couldn't have been written. I would like to thank Mark Solms, George Makari, and Asti Hustvedt for their careful reading of and commentary on the manuscript of *The Shaking Woman*, and, finally, I am grateful to my husband, Paul Auster, not only for reading this text, but for his patience. For years, he has kindly tolerated my passionate immersion in the brain/mind problem and listened to me think aloud (sometimes for hours) about many of the issues I address in this book.

SIRI HUSTVEDT

A Plea for Eros

In this illuminating and absorbing collection of essays, Siri Hustvedt explores many of the themes that preoccupy her novels: identity and memory, sexuality and mortality, psychology, love and the power of imagination. But here she offers her personal experience – as daughter, sister, mother and wife, student, reader and writer – to illustrate these fundamental aspects of our lives. Wise, honest and luminously intelligent, this is a book that invites us to look afresh at ourselves and the universe we inhabit.

'She strides across these pages ... Hustvedt is a lucid writer, whose spare, elegant prose wears lightly its eclectic reference points.'
Observer

'Thoughtful, sensuous essays ... her enthusiasms are oddly infectious'
Daily Telegraph

'An intellectual, emotional and elegantly written collection that leaves the reader with plenty to ponder ... Her passion for language and literature makes the prose leap from the page ... Hustvedt is, quite simply, an extraordinary literary talent. Read it, ponder it, then go read it again.'
Image

'A luminous collection of mind-expanding pieces on literary and philosophical themes ... A book to renew one's faith in the literary essay' Robert McCrum, *Observer*

SCEPTRE

SIRI HUSTVEDT

What I Loved

In 1975, art historian Leo Hertzberg discovers an extraordinary painting by an unknown artist in a New York gallery. He buys the work, tracks down its creator, Bill Weschler, and the two men embark on a life-long friendship. This is the story of their intense and troubled relationship, of the women in their lives and the nature of love and seduction, of their work, of art and hysteria, and of their sons – born the same year but whose lives take very different paths.

'A love story with the grip and suspense of a thriller.
It makes you ponder human existence with a peculiar
mixture of stoicism and wonder'
Times Literary Supplement

'A big, wide, sensuous novel – clever,
sinister, yet attractively real'
Guardian

'Truly memorable' *Sunday Times*

'Substantial, moving and beautifully written'
Independent on Sunday

'Riveting ... rich, densely textured and utterly absorbing'
Lesley Glaister

'Subtle, compassionate, wise' *Time Out*

'Consummately intelligent ... intensely moving' *Scotsman*

'Clever and engaging' *Observer*

'Eerie and atmospheric' *Daily Telegraph*

SCEPTRE

SIRI HUSTVEDT

The Sorrows of an American

My sister called it 'the year of secrets,' but when I look back on it now, I've come to understand that it was a time not of what was there, but of what wasn't.

'It is a rare writer who can both rouse the mind and grip the heart, and all the while provide the sensuous delights of image and language ... a compelling narrative in which the past haunts the present of characters so vividly real they become members of your intimate circle and erupt in your dreams ... almost impossible to put down, and even harder not to re-read'
Lisa Appignanesi, *Independent*

'Wonderful' *Observer*

'Astonishing ... Hustvedt is famous for writing positively thrilling prose. But she is on fire here ... This passionately conceived, coolly delivered work is almost certainly the best American novel you will read this year.'
Sunday Telegraph

'Subtle and complex ... Hustvedt switches gracefully between her characters, involving them in each other's webs of grief and secrecy, confession and anger, lust and need'
Sunday Times

'One of the most profound and absorbing books I've read in a long time ... I reached the end emotionally and intellectually exhausted, knowing how much I'll miss this book'
Washington Post

'Beautifully thought through, deeply serious and enormously intelligent'
Jane Smiley, *Guardian*

SCEPTRE